Intensive Interaction

Education at SAGE

SAGE is a leading international publisher of journals, books, and electronic media for academic, educational, and professional markets.

Our education publishing includes:

- accessible and comprehensive texts for aspiring education professionals and practitioners looking to further their careers through continuing professional development

- inspirational advice and guidance for the classroom

- authoritative state of the art reference from the leading authors in the field

Find out more at: **www.sagepub.co.uk/education**

Intensive
Interaction

Theoretical Perspectives

Edited by Dave Hewett

Los Angeles | London | New Delhi
Singapore | Washington DC

SAGE Publications Ltd
1 Oliver's Yard
55 City Road
London EC1Y 1SP

SAGE Publications Inc.
2455 Teller Road
Thousand Oaks, California 91320

SAGE Publications India Pvt Ltd
B 1/I 1 Mohan Cooperative Industrial Area
Mathura Road
New Delhi 110 044

SAGE Publications Asia-Pacific Pte Ltd
33 Pekin Street #02–01
Far East Square
Singapore 048763

Library of Congress Control Number: 2011923248

British Library Cataloguing in Publication data

A catalogue record for this book is available from the British Library

ISBN 978-0-85702-170-0
ISBN 978-0-85702-171-7 (pbk)

Typeset by Dorwyn, Wells, Somerset
Printed in India by Replika Press Pvt Ltd
Printed on paper from sustainable resources

Contents

About the editor and contributors

Editor

Dave Hewett has been working in the field of special education for 35 years. He was headteacher at Harperbury Hospital School throughout the 1980s, where the team worked on the development and first research on Intensive Interaction. With Melanie Nind he produced the first Intensive Interaction book in 1994. Since 1990 he has been an independent consultant, continuing to publish and work on the development and dissemination of the approach. He is now Director of the Intensive Interaction Institute, broadcasting Intensive Interaction increasingly worldwide.

Contributors

Mark Barber worked in the UK as a special educator for 20 years before moving to Australia, where he has introduced Intensive Interaction to over 90 schools and services for learners with severe-profound intellectual disabilities. Mark currently divides his time between working as Intensive Interaction Coordinator and Leading Teacher at Bayside Special Developmental School in Melbourne and working as a consultant in profound intellectual disability, providing training and support to schools and practitioners in a variety of settings. He coordinates Intensive Interaction across Australia and New Zealand.

Graham Firth is Intensive Interaction Project Leader at Leeds Partnerships NHS Trust. In the 1980s Graham worked for six years as a care assistant at a large residential hospital for adults with learning disabilities in Leeds (UK), before leaving to pursue a career in teaching. Initially spending several years working in primary schools, Graham then went on to teach adults with severe or profound learning disabilities. After becoming dissatisfied with the then asocial pedagogy, he started to work more interactively before formally adopting Intensive Interaction as his main teaching strategy. In 2003 he joined the Leeds Partnerships NHS Trust, where he now works to support others to adopt, sustain and develop their Intensive Interaction practices or services. He is currently the editor of the *UK Intensive Interaction Newsletter* and the Leeds Partnership NHS Trust's Intensive Interaction webpage (at www.leedspft.nhs.uk), and is a member of the trust's Severe Challenging Behaviour Team.

Cath Irvine qualified as a speech and language therapist in 1991 from Manchester Polytechnic (now Manchester Metropolitan University). After three years in a generalist post, Cath began to specialise in learning disabilities working in Wirral, Salford and Somerset. In 1996 Cath was instrumental in introducing Intensive Interaction to adult services across Somerset. Since 2005 Cath has worked independently introducing Intensive Interaction to services in the UK, Montenegro, Moldova and Bulgaria. Cath is a co-director of the Intensive Interaction Institute and is constantly active in seeking practical and strategic solutions for the increased use of Intensive Interaction for those who would benefit.

Penny Lacey is a senior lecturer at the University of Birmingham for four days a week and an adviser in a special school for primary-aged children with learning difficulties for the fifth day. She has been associated with interactive approaches to teaching and learning since the 1980s, having written extensively on different aspects of the topic for 25 years. At the university, Penny coordinates the distance education programme Learning Difficulties and Disabilities (Severe, Profound and Complex) which attracts students from all around the country and abroad. She also conducts research in the area of education for children with severe and profound disabilities. At school she is supporting staff to develop provision for the most profoundly disabled children.

Melanie Nind is Professor of Education at the University of Southampton. Her expertise lies in the fields of interactive and inclusive pedagogy. She is best known for her work developing and evaluating Intensive Interaction. She has taught in special schools and further education colleges, before working in the Centre for Autism Studies at the University of Hertfordshire, Oxford Brookes University and the Open University developing and teaching undergraduate and postgraduate courses in inclusive education. Her recent research has focused on education for girls with behavioural, emotional and social difficulties; understanding and developing the concept of access for people with learning difficulties; and studying the interactions of young children with learning difficulties in special, inclusive and home environments. She maintains a keen interest in gender, sexuality and disability rights issues within a broad social justice framework. She is editor of the *International Journal of Research and Method in Education*.

Lydia Swinton has worked in the field of special needs for nine years, following the completion of a psychology degree in 2000. In 2005 Lydia qualified as a teacher, and completed her MA in special and inclusive education in 2009. The application of Intensive Interaction with students with autistic spectrum disorder was the subject of her MA dissertation. Lydia is currently a senior teacher at Sunfield School, West Midlands.

Dr M. Suzanne Zeedyk is Senior Lecturer in Developmental Psychology at the University of Dundee. She has spent the past 20 years researching the nature of human communication, focusing particularly on the early interactions between parents and infants. She is excited by the recent neuroscientific findings that show the infant brain is literally moulded by these early emotional exchanges, and she spends much of her time these days disseminating that knowledge to the public.

Acknowledgements

So many people contribute in multifarious ways to a book such as this that it is difficult to know where to start making acknowledgements. Additionally, most of the people I would usually have mentioned as major influences or supporters are contributing to the book. Nonetheless I will indulge some editor privileges.

In the Introduction I make special mention of Sarah Forde, who runs the Intensive Interaction office. Likewise, Jude Bowen, Alex Molineux and Amy Jarrold at Sage have been, and I believe there is no higher word of praise, optimum.

I would like to make a particularly personal mention of Vanessa and Philip Bingham, who offered a tranquil and creative haven in Tianjin, China at a time when the very first steps in commencing the project seemed particularly daunting.

I would also like to thank Jan Gordon, Ian Harris, Helen Janes, Carol Jones, Jacci Kellett, Uwe Kerat, Miranda-Jane McCormick, Lynette Menzies, Julia Rhodes, Gunter Senft, Emily Seyler, Ben Smith, Ellen Winter.

Introduction

The development and dissemination of Intensive Interaction is surely illuminated by the fact that all the major proponents are people who are first and foremost practitioners, but practitioners also entranced by the theoretical aspects of what they do. They have been gradually offering a growing and developing body of literature supporting Intensive Interaction. Here is some more for your enjoyment. This book is a pleasurable project I have had in mind for some time but for various reasons I have been delayed in embarking upon it.

For some of the contributions here, any delay has enabled their time, perhaps more comfortably, to arrive. I am thinking particularly of the survey of pertinent neurology described by M. Suzanne Zeedyk. Owing to the fast-developing nature of knowledge in that field, her chapter can probably be more insightfully penned at this time than, say, even five years ago. Suzanne's work is probably known to all of you who open this book and she was the first name in my mind when thinking about a chapter on the neural development implications of doing Intensive Interaction.

For well over 20 years I have regarded Penny Lacey with an awe that does not diminish with knowing her better. Among all of the noted authorities in the special needs field, Penny is surely the one best known for her clear insights and straightforward pronouncements. Here, Penny has added another layer of conceptualisation to groundbreaking thinking on curriculum and teaching approaches that she commenced more than those 20 years ago.

Similarly, my 'teacher head' used the space available to me to write up some thoughts on curriculum theory and learning structures that I have been working with for some years, but not yet put into print. I sincerely hope that all in the educational field who have the need can recognise that there is a well-described curriculum rationale for

Intensive Interaction. I hope, too, it can be seen that this rationale both embraces the existence of Intensive Interaction and points the way to the further acceptance and use of emergent learning models together with the development of other interactive and 'process central' teaching approaches.

For other topics, the detailed description or setting out of our thinking is perhaps overdue. One such would be Melanie Nind's survey of the likely emotional development that is brought about for the learner as a result of Intensive Interaction activities. Mel and I have discussed the prospect that, in our previous books together, we have not placed enough emphasis in this outcomes area. We quickly saw that this project was one opportunity to address this oversight.

In a similar vein, Lydia Swinton's chapter probably should have been published 10 or 15 years ago. I have been admiring Lydia's gifts in her work with teenagers who have autistic spectrum disorder (ASD) for the last seven years or so. We have never particularly trumpeted Intensive Interaction as an 'autism intervention'. Indeed, it is not specifically that. It is an approach that works well for people who are at a certain levels of development – that includes many people who have ASD. However, when Melanie and I were working with our team on the development of the approach throughout the 1980s, probably around half of our adult students were people with ASD. I suggest there are many senses in which during its development, Intensive Interaction became beautifully tailored to the learning and lifestyle needs of people on the spectrum, indeed, in which it focuses on some of the central effects of their condition. I expect Lydia's work will assist many autism specialist practitioners and establishments who currently do not work in this way, to become alive to this reality.

The chapters by Graham Firth, Mark Barber and Cath Irvine are representative of the creative thinking that branches out in various theoretical directions as a result of involvement in the simple human practicalities of the approach. These three remarkable people are a prime example of those who are first and foremost practitioners, noteworthy to this day for their alacrity with being 'on the floor and playing'. They are noteworthy too for being learned, deep-thinking authors on our approach.

Even though I spend quite a bit of time with him, I cannot work out how Graham runs the Leeds Intensive Interaction Project, organises conferences, gives courses, publishes the newsletter, goes to the Interactive Café, has an enviable family life *and* seems calm and composed at all times. Cath equally exudes a sense of international dash these days, shuttling frequently between the UK and all her support work in eastern Europe. Mark, fortunately, is a 'big' communicator, contributing all the way from his base in Melbourne, where he has single-handedly led the way in generating Intensive Interaction work in Australia.

So, we welcome you to *Intensive Interaction: Theoretical Perspectives*. The first chapter relates Intensive Interaction to some general, crucial communication matters affecting all of us. It is attempted within it to bring out a sense of 'connectedness' to subsequent chapters. Indeed, I do hope readers will experience a continuing sense of inter-connectedness throughout the book, even though each chapter is apparently on a different topic.

Finally, I would like to thank Jude Bowen, Alex Molineux and Amy Jarrold at Sage for their enthusiasm and total, positive support during this project. Thanks and recognition above all to Sarah Forde for her continuous, unstinting effort in background work over all these years, that makes it possible for the rest of us to do what we do.

Dave Hewett
Malvern, January 2011

1

Blind frogs: the nature of human communication and Intensive Interaction

Dave Hewett

> ## Chapter overview
>
> This chapter refers to the complexity of interpersonal communications and the often non-conscious cognitions that support them. It emphasises too, the essentially pleasurable, discursive and goal-free nature of most of our interactions. This will be described with reference to communication theory and related to Intensive Interaction and the present nature of communication work in the field of learning difficulty.

Blind frogs

I have a video clip that I use during various courses. I have been using the clip for three or four years as a stimulus for a group discussion about the nature of human communication. I show it with the sound turned off, for good reasons which I will explain. I ask the group to watch it first and foremost with enjoyment. Secondly, I ask them to feel free to have big and analytical thoughts about human communication and to share them as we watch. I will describe what takes place in the video clip. It lasts about 4 minutes.

There are five women sitting or standing in a clearly relaxed social group. They range in age from about 25 to 50 years. It seems obvious that they know each other well. They are in what looks like a class-room or actually a playroom and I think you gradually realise that it is likely they are practitioners in our field who are on a break.

They are socially 'lit-up'. They are talking in one group, smiling and laughing a lot, referencing to each other quite excitedly both ver-bally and non-verbally. Gradually it becomes clear that one of them, Ellen, is telling a story. The others slow down somewhat and become more still, though they comment and interject, clearly adding humorously to what Ellen is describing. Ellen obviously has racon-teur skills and is enjoying her story, indeed painting a picture with mime and deliberate flourishes of gesture and facial expressions.

Gradually, the interaction between them lifts off again – more smil-ing and giggling, more interjections from all five followed by pauses for outright belly laughing and much more vivid non-verbals by everybody. It looks like they are all being humorously creative and are completely in tune with each other, exchanging rapid, intense eye contacts, facial expressions, body language and gesture. It also looks like it would be noisy if I turned the sound up.

Gradually, my group will start making observations about the ele-ments of human communication they are observing in the video. Having the sound turned off facilitates their observation of the importance of the non-verbal exchange between the five people. This was one of my original intentions in using the clip. Usually, group members will talk about the eye contacts, how many and var-ious they are, how intently they study each others' faces and eyes, questing to read each others' emotional and psychological flows in the visual information they are picking up from each other.

Links

In Chapter 5, Lydia Swinton reviews the difficulties people who have a diagnosis of autism can have in learning and taking part in these ordi-nary human experiences.

I like to develop these observations into discussion about the deep exchange taking place. I observe the significance, the profundity, the complexity of the non-verbals; the reading of faces, eyes and body language. Each person is demonstrating this profound ability to 'face and mind read' the other person, make moment-by-moment assumptions about the other person's inner state, enhancing the sense of emotional and psychological connection. The greater component of a communication exchange is not the speech, it is the non-verbals, by far.

These abilities we remind ourselves, are among the most complicated learning that human beings do. It is also part of the first learning, commenced from day one. The group discussion can then range to the challenge of Intensive Interaction. Our approach focuses on teaching these things, and all other incredibly complex fundamentals, including all the vocal attainments up to and including speech, to the people who have the most severe learning difficulties.

With the video clip set on slow motion to aid observation, we can start to perceive and talk about an aspect of being a communicator that it is literally difficult to bring into one's awareness. This is the prospect that these intricate non-verbal exchanges are not fully conscious to the participants and fall within the realm of what Lakin (2006) terms, 'automatic cognitive processes'.

In the literature on these things, there is a developing focus on the likely reality that large aspects of intricate communicative interplay are dealt with by one's non-consciousness.[1] In large part it is a non-conscious operation that deals with the reception and processing of information from the incredible array of minute signals, for instance, from another person's face. If I understand Lakin and also Dijksterhuis and Nordgren (2006) correctly, they propose that consciousness has a limited capacity for processing that sort of information – one might say the consciousness does not have sufficient random access memory (RAM). Rather, in non-verbal processing, the non-conscious mind deals with these complexities at high speed and then feeds the results back into conscious thought as an array of sort, of intuitive awarenesses that assist with your understanding of and sense of connection with, the other person. (If this brief account tickles your curiosity, I do recommend reading the already cited Jessica Lakin. I propose that this is an area of our work to which we should and will, in future, be paying much more attention.)

'Of course,' we in the group all then cry, that is why Intensive Interaction is a free-flowing process-central approach! It has to be like that in order to allow for the teaching and learning of all the non-conscious components of communication performance! You cannot task-analyse these components, you cannot even comprehend them within your own mind.

> ↻ **Link**
>
> For further discussion of these issues, see Chapter 9, 'What is Intensive Interaction? Curriculum, process and approach', by Dave Hewett.

Goleman (2006: 16) refers to this neural circuitry 'that operates beneath our awareness' as the 'low road'. We are consciously aware of the 'high road' that 'runs through neural systems which work more methodically, step-by-step and with more deliberate effort'. He takes the computer analogy even further than I by referring to people indulging 'neural wi-fi' in their non-conscious communicative connections. He also describes the neuroscience term, 'empathic resonance' – the parallel triggering of neural circuitry, particularly mirror neurons, in two people communicating and relating.

> ↻ **Link**
>
> M. Suzanne Zeedyk overviews neural development and communication in Chapter 4.

So, I think we can observe Ellen and the others indulging in face and mind-reading, neural wi-fi and empathic resonance via the low road. They also seem to be having a wonderful, enjoyable time doing it. In fact, somewhere during the discussion, a group member will usually observe that we should not forget what simple human joy Ellen and her friends are visibly experiencing.

Next, I ask, can anyone make a guess at what these people are talking about? There are many amusing suggestions, but I assure them that (a) they will never guess it and (b) if it is not already obvious, they are definitely not talking about anything sensible.

I explain. At the weekend, Ellen and her husband at long last found an afternoon for cleaning out their long-murky garden pond. At the bottom of the pond they found a great deal of filthy ooze. In the ooze they astonishingly found many, pale-skinned, blind-seeming frogs, piled up on and coiled around one another. As Ellen is relating this, the others have their imaginations fired up and start making all sorts of fanciful suggestions for how they got there. They start trying to imagine the blind frog exodus that arrived one summer evening in Ellen's garden when they were evicted from elsewhere. Someone suggests perhaps they come out of the pond for moonlit frog country-dancing. Another group member suggests that perhaps they are alien frogs occupying all the ponds in Surrey – they will rise up one dank evening and take over the world, and so on.

I allowed a hundred words or so to describe their discussion for a reason. I know these people very well; they are intelligent, capable, cultured people. But they were quite happy to spend 4 minutes with their imaginations taking flight and talking absolute rubbish to each other in a happy sharing. As you might guess, this was not the first time.

The functions and content of human communications

Think about it. Think about all of your conversations every day with the people around you in all circumstances. It might be useful, first, to think about a day when you are not at work, though it is very interesting to consider work circumstances too.

How many of the things said to each other, when you really consider it, actually needed to be said? Lots of course, but many, maybe most of your utterances or conversations, will have no tangible outcome or purpose – nothing concrete happens because of them. I am not claiming that these sorts of communications are in any way unimportant, far from it, but nearly all of them are a sort of rubbish that does not need to be aired: 'Brightened up again hasn't it?' 'Did you see it last night?' 'No, I didn't vote for him, didn't like his Tango.' 'I'm just off to the loo.' 'Have you heard what Irene did?' 'We went to the Safari Park at the weekend.' 'How's it going?'

As stated, these conversations are apparently trivial, but that does not mean they are unimportant. In fact, as I will explore, they fulfil a very deep and rich function for all of us, maybe the deepest and most meaningful function there is. I think about them as the hot air of human companionship. I think my five friends talking about blind frogs for four hilarious minutes was a good example of the hot air of companionship. The examples I listed above are 'blind frogs' types of communications.

Blind frogs communications (let us call them BFs from now on for brevity) in my conceptualisation, would include all conversations, or indeed other interactions such as non-verbal banter, that do not have some sort of extrinsic, instrumental, concrete aim or outcome;

conversations that are therefore apparently purposeless. I estimate I would include everything we categorise, for instance, as:

- small talk
- chit-chat
- gossiping
- banter
- chewing the cud
- chewing the fat
- doing the craic.

Let us call communications that do have a concrete aim or outcome CCAOs for brevity. Examples of CCAOs would be: 'Would it be possible to extend my overdraft?' 'Have you got it in a 16?' 'Just put it over there please.' 'Not today thank you.' 'You wash, I'll dry.' We would also include all of the complicated and necessarily goal-directed meetings, discussions and other interactions that are needed during our work. Goal-orientated, outcomes-orientated communications are necessary, too, for constructing the education system, the World Bank, the European monetary system, politics, sending spaceships to the moon, running factories, organising society, technology and culture. Then there are communications familiar to us in our field, our work communications where we are helping people. The communications where we attempt to encourage someone to complete a table-top task, to wash their own face, to respond to questions or do things: 'Would you like orange juice?' 'What colour is this?' 'Up you get ... up.' 'Say hello to ... Aaron.'

Texts on communication theories provide many other ways of categorising human communication and conversation. For the purposes of this chapter, I will use only these two categories: BF and CCAO. Actually, I think that often, even when we are doing CCAOs, we have as many BFs as possible in there as part of the process. How many of us simmer during meetings as people indulge too many BFs when the meeting should be getting on with the CCAO that is the purpose?

I will describe some BFs. The following is nearly the most enjoyable thing in my life. It is not my work. I like to cook, I like to entertain, I like to drink wine and I like to talk, converse. I love dinner parties and I have them as frequently as I can. I had five friends over – these are intelligent, sophisticated people, I judge. I cooked far too much food. We all brought to the table a shameful quantity of wine. We sat in my conservatory at the dining table for 5 to 6 hours. We had wonderful music. We ate all of the food, gradually. We drank most of the wine. We talked and laughed hilariously and I believe, intelligently for all of that time, though most of it probably falls into the category of humorous rubbish – actually, the craic. I do not think any of us said anything that brought about a concrete outcome of any sort, other than 'pass the salt please', or something similar. There was, however, I believe, the reinforcing sense of human connection and fulfilling relationship we all took away from the table.

Try to think deeply about all your BFs. What are they for? What do they do? Why are we so committed to having them? Try to imagine your life without them happening. I cannot conceive of what my life would be like if I could not indulge in those social gatherings like my dinner party and all of the other thousands of briefer, incidental, purely discursive social incidents that come my way each day.

It already seems to be a cliché to refer to Twitter as an example of anything, but surely this is a case in point. What is Twitter for? A study (Kelly, 2009) by an admitted Twitter enthusiast (beware, probably not too scientific, but quite well framed) analysed Tweets and found that:

- 40.55 per cent of were total, pointless babble

- 37.55 per cent were conversational (this could include polls, so there may be some CCAOs hiding in there).

I have increasingly come round to the point of view that the main function of human communication is actually to have blind frogs-type interactions and accrue the sense of well-being that arises from these experiences. As it happens, perhaps due to evolutionary accidents (Dunbar, 1996, 1998, for instance, proposes the social gossip theory of evolution) humans have become so sophisticated as communicators that we can use our communication abilities for all those other, practical, important, extrinsic outcomes – the CCAOs, that other animal species struggle with. 'I suggest, then that the principal function of language was (and still is) to enable the exchange of social information (gossip) in order to facilitate the bonding in larger, more dispersed social groups' (Dunbar 1998: 98).

Important as all CCAOs are, of course, those who study these matters will usually conclude in various ways that what I am terming CCAOs make up the *smaller* proportion of our daily communications with one another. Dunbar (1996), describing a study that actually did not focus on the totality of what I term BFs, found that around 65 per cent of speaking time was taken up with talking about social experiences of one sort or another. This figure concurs with a similar finding by Emler (1992). Emler and Dunbar, of course, focus in their studies on what they term 'gossip'. However, as Baumeister et al. (2004) and McAndrew (2008) emphasise, we do not necessarily connotate from that the solely negative implication of malicious gossip. Rather, there is an implication of gossip as general social exchange, with the main content being social and about *people*.

There is an irresistible link here to an area of study which crosses boundaries between anthropology and psycholinguistics, but is still perhaps struggling to gain a profile in psychology and education. 'Phatic' communications are defined somewhat variously but usually as something like: 'communications where what is said is less important than the fact that something is said at all' (Pearce, 1989: 97). During Internet searching, I was much attracted to this definition for its conciseness: 'conversational speech used to communicate sociability more than information' (Princeton University, 2006).

Senft (2009: 228) writes that phatic communications are 'utterances that are said to have exclusively social, bonding functions like establishing and maintaining a friendly and harmonious atmosphere in interpersonal relations, especially during the opening and closing stages of social-verbal-encounters'. Senft eloquently reviews the work of the originator of the term, anthropologist Bronislaw Malinowski (1923): 'phatic communion serves to establish bonds of personal union between people brought together by the mere need of companionship and does not serve any purpose of communicating ideas' (2009: 316). Note that Malinowski's original formulation employed the term 'communion'. The application of the word 'communication' has been a later modification by others that has gradually become the commonly accepted term. Senft is keen to point out the religious connotation of this word with its effect of emphasising the intensity of this type of communication. I would also celebrate the use of the word and its atmosphere of coming together in social union, a sense of everyday connection that is nonetheless almost spiritual in emotional and psychological importance to the participants. In effect, this is the central theme of my chapter.

Adler and Rodman (2006: 9–10) list four functions of human communication. It fulfils:

Physical needs
'Communication is so important that it is necessary for physical health. In fact, evidence suggests that an absence of satisfying communications can even jeopardize life itself ... personal communication is essential for our well-being.'

Identity needs
'Communication does more than enable us to survive. It is the way, indeed the *only* way ... we learn who we are ... our sense of identity comes from the way we interact with other people.'

Social needs
These include 'pleasure', 'affection', 'inclusion', 'escape', 'relaxation' and 'control'. Furthermore, 'imagine how empty your life would be if these needs weren't satisfied.'

Practical needs
'Everyday important functions ... the tool that lets us tell the hair stylist to take just a little off the sides, direct the doctor to where it hurts ... etc.'

I suggest you can identify that three of the four categories of human need listed above will be served by all people simply having a plentiful supply of BFs. The essential point here is that 'personal communication is essential for our well-being' (Adler and Rodman, 2006: 10) and it may be that communication is the 'primary goal' of human existence (Adler and Rodman, 2006: 11).

I believe I can identify from my experiences of having the blind frogs video discussion on a number of occasions that what I am outlining here about our everyday reality falls into the realm of 'oh yes, I'd never thought about it that way', for most people. Practitioners considering the issues for the first time tend to have a rather big moment of realisation about the nature of communication, often with corresponding deep thought about the implications for their practice, which we will come to in the next section.

For all of us, our sense of internal well-being will vary enormously from individual to individual. However, for each one of us, what is the main source of our internal sense of goodness and well-being? Surely, the main source is not our achievements, our qualifications, the increasing development of our skills and performances, our increasing wealth or, even, that other people *tell* you that you are a good person. Is not the main source of well-being the simple, mostly unspoken quality and quantity of our fulfilling relationships and communications with everyone around us? This particularly, but not exclusively, includes our nearest and dearest. It makes me feel pretty good about myself that the five marvellous, talented, lovely people at my dinner table wish to spend time with me, for no reward other than the time spent. Moreover, they are five people who do this with me frequently, so it was not an accident nor a one-off. This simple inner knowledge helps enormously during times when life confronts me with the reality of my frailties or lesser qualities.

↻↺ Link

See Chapter 2, 'Intensive Interaction, emotional development and emotional well-being', by Melanie Nind.

Again, can we all try to imagine what sort of person we might be if we did not have this surely gigantic supply of BFs? What would life be like if your communications were restricted to: 'A cup of tea please.' 'Two returns to Waterloo please.' 'Any other items for the agenda?'

Michael Rutter is known for his work on attachment and maternal deprivation (Rutter, 1972). Rutter and Rutter (1993) suggest that if attachment is thought of in terms of the kinds of relationships that provide deep emotional support and reduce anxiety, it seems clear that attachment is in evidence though all stages of life, including old age. I suggest you can see this in people around you at these various stages. I think you can see also that where people – anyone you know – lack for whatever reason, big, significant, ongoing bonded relationships, they will find many various sources of support in their other relationships and interactions.

Burton and Dimbleby (1995: 6–7) argue the critical role of communication in establishing and maintaining a sense of self, that an attractive self only becomes apparent when it communicates with others. Further, that one's sense of self-image must be 'in a dynamic relationship with the outside world' and that the 'link with the outside world is communication'. Self-esteem is a variable factor where its 'degree' relates to our use of communication. 'But even now it must be apparent that communication is a crucial bridge between ourselves and others. We can only be known through our communication' (Burton and Dimbleby, 1995: 5).

So, to reiterate and conclude this section. After I think, a great deal of thought, discussion and reading on the matter outlined in the last few paragraphs, I believe I understand the following. The positive human outcomes outlined in the last few paragraphs are, of course, dependent on the quality and quantity of the communications that a person receives or takes part in. It therefore seems obvious that a large quantity of BF experiences are absolutely critical for any person. It seems clear that the well-being issues outlined here cannot be supplied by a large quantity of communications with a concrete aim or outcome alone. Indeed, it is suggested that an imbalance in types of communication, for example many more CCAOs than BFs, will actually be harmful, to all of us, but especially to people who are still at early stages of development communicatively, psychologically and emotionally.

How is this way of viewing human communications reflected in our work?

Jim, a psychologist friend and colleague of mine, has recently been stunned into several months of deep thought about blind frogs. He has had, by his own admission, one of those previously mentioned 'Wow, I've never thought about it like that', moments. The meeting was discussing ways to address the needs of a young, adult woman in one of the services Jim supports; let us call her Julie. Julie's internal state and behaviour were clearly deeply distressed. The biggest suggestion during discussion about factors contributing to her state was that she was desperately lonely and isolated and she needed more attention from members of staff. Not just any old attention, she needed loads of blind frogs-type attention. Interactions just for the sake of it. No task, no aim, no outcome that the moments are driving towards, just the simple, basic, lovely human reward of another person conversing or interacting with you just for the sake of being with you – and frequently. Those of us in the meeting entertained the prospect that this might contribute highly positively to her behaviour and state of being. The team members present were commendably clear and candid about the present state of Julie's communication environment.

> ↶↷ **Link**
>
> In Chapter 8 Cath Irvine surveys issues concerned with embedding Intensive Interaction awareness and practice within services.

It may already be clear that part of my main concern in this chapter is that the simple human experiences that I just described as being necessary for Julie needed to be outlined in an action plan, as an intervention, in order for her to receive them. These are the simple, basic, ordinary everyday BF experiences that nearly all of us receive in large quantities every day – but not Julie, unless we planned it.

There are very good reasons for this state of affairs that I believe I do understand (don't we all?) and there is no criticism of the team around Julie; I think they are rather fine actually.

I therefore feel I need to make a further apologetic qualification before proceeding in this section. I am inevitably about to make critical observations about practices in our field of work. I do this, not unusually, in my working life and I am always careful to stipulate that I do not exclude myself. Over the years I have been there, done that – and worse. Mostly, I experience feelings of awe about the wonderfulness of the teams and practitioners I meet, and the way in which they can continue doing what they do in often pretty daunting circumstances. Plus, as I said, I believe I understand the reasons why our often standard practices are the way that they are. But, of course, I am hoping always to point towards positive horizons as I make the critique.

My main thought is that people with severe learning difficulty (SLD) and autistic spectrum disorder (ASD) in our services, both schools and adult services, may receive a lot of staff attention and interaction. However, the by far greater proportion of that attention is likely to be task orientated, goal directed, intended to achieve an instrumental outcome and with the member of staff leading, directing and following a predetermined agenda. There is nothing wrong with that for achieving all sorts of things, of course, but the problems come when most of a person's interactions with members of staff are CCAOs, and BFs are few. This problem is heightened when the person is an adult living in a staffed house and does not have abilities concomitant with interacting socially with other residents.

Studies in this area are actually limited, mostly within adult services, and most of the writers refer to the need for more observations. The studies quoted do offer more than the simple categorisation of communication routines that I use here. I will keep this literature review brief – I have no desire to present some sort of catalogue of woe. However, I would ask the reader to consider positively whether what is outlined rings bells of familiarity.

To put it in the sort of nomenclature used in such studies, they tend to find, for instance, that functional communications by staff were more prevalent than social or conversational interactions (Markova et al., 1992). Most speech utterances by staff to service users were directives (McConkey et al., 1999) or comments and requests (Bradshaw, 2001a; Zilber et al., 1994); or question pursuit (Antaki et al., 2007). Overall staff contact with service users was very low (Bradshaw, 2001a).

↻↺ Link

Read more in Chapter 7, by Graham Firth, 'Intensive Interaction for inclusion and development'.

McConkey et al. (1999) recommend some key topics for staff training arising from their observations of staff-service user interactions:

- matching their language to clients' understanding

- increased use of non-verbal signals

- use of more open questions

- providing opportunities for the client to initiate topics

- increased responsiveness.

I thoroughly recommend Bradshaw's (2001b) paper for its extensive review and for pointing the way towards 'communication partnerships'. Herein lies a practical model for staff communication practice, accessible theoretical and practical guidance. Indeed, I suggest, although a decade or more has passed, it seems to me that the views and recommendations of both of these latter papers are still current, that practices on communication have not moved on greatly in many places during this time, and that the recommendations and guidelines offered are therefore still positive prospects. I must also recommend viewing the optimistic and forward-looking model for general staff training on these issues being currently developed in Finland (Martikainen and Roisko, 2004, cited in Koski et al., 2010).

As a former special school headteacher I naturally feel the greatest immediate empathy with the many (desperately) dedicated classroom staff I work with each year. In 1994, psychologist John Harris made observations along the lines that in his view, standard practices and interaction routines in special school classrooms were more likely to inhibit the development of the pupils' communication abilities than enhance (Harris, 1994). I find, when I am in schools, that John Harris's observation stays quite prominently in my mind. It haunts me somewhat. Ware (1996) wrote a whole, lovely, helpful book dedicated to helping classroom teams get these things into some area of 'rightness'. It is particularly focused on children with profound and multiple leaning difficulties, but its advice is highly generalisable to people with SLD. Once again, I feel that these observations and the advice offered in these two works can still be current in some areas or establishments. Of course, during the past 15 years, the uptake and implementation of Intensive Interaction in education points towards what I would naturally consider to be huge moves in the right direction. But I am nonetheless still haunted by John Harris's observation.

> ↻ **Link**
>
> Penny Lacey (Chapter 3) provides authoritative further reading on the nature of interactive approaches within special education curricula.

Other than Intensive Interaction, if you look at approaches to the teaching of communication that are in most popular and widespread use, they are all focused on teaching CCAOs. They tend to focus on teaching the use of CCAOs *by* the use of CCAOs. In a general sense, I believe there is still a lot to do in order to generate an awareness that there is more to communication for pupils and service users (well, for all people of course) than requesting drinks or other basic needs. Please be clear, I am not disregarding the need for nor the benefits of teaching those communication attainments to the people who can learn them (I find myself saying this frequently). I am in no way wishing to be critical of or diminish a practitioner's zeal to teach a child something concrete and clearly ostensibly useful.

> ↻ **Link**
>
> Mark Barber (Chapter 6) extensively discusses these issues – the relative pertinence of our various approaches to communication teaching.

However, the above is an observation about the, I believe, still general unawareness in our system of the crucial, and actually greater importance of phatic communication. Intensive Interaction aside, there seems to be little technical knowledge about how to help pupils with SLD learn phatic and general social communication. I do see widespread incidental, undocumented work happening *outside* the curriculum through the intuitive behaviour of wonderful practitioners that I see everywhere. However, an implication of Harris's (1994) observation would be, I believe, that many of our standard ways of working can often, mostly, inhibit the natural human interactions that achieve this. This chapter has simply sought to illustrate this issue. Actually, with a sort of happy perversity, considering what I just wrote, I look forward to a time actually when we do not have something called 'Intensive Interaction'. The practices will be so standard, so blended-in, that we will forget to call it anything.

☐ Summary

So in, I think, proper style for this book, I should bring the discussion back to Intensive Interaction in order to conclude. I believe the issues of phatic communication outlined in this chapter have always been addressed within Intensive Interaction practices – often, I guess, unknowingly. I think that we did not address the issues with enough emphasis in our first book on Intensive Interaction (Nind and Hewett, 1994), simply because our thinking now is more extensive and informed than then. In various ways, the issues were somewhat more prominent in the subsequent, edited volume (Hewett and Nind, 1998). The production of this volume is an opportunity to redress any lack of previous emphasis, but also to relate these observations to work in various fields that has occurred *since* 1994. I strongly sug-gest that the issue of phatic communication is literally the most important one in the lives of the people we are thinking about here. This perspective does not raise its head much in our field, though there is some discussion of the issue in the field of mental health nurs-ing (for example, see Burnard, 2003).

Back, then, to Jim's meeting. There was discussion as to how Julie could be given a plentiful supply of blind frog experiences, since she is a person at an early level of development as a communicator and does not relate with easy facility. One of the outcomes to the meet-ing was that the team would receive training in Intensive Interaction.

Intensive Interaction is actually phatic communication – no, *com-munion* – or it is, I think, to the participants, during the moments of their participation. The ultimate outcomes of course, of Intensive Interaction, or let us use, rather, the natural model of parent–infant interaction, are anything but phatic. The whole, overall process might be viewed as working towards crucial, predictable, concrete outcomes – the complete development of communication abilities. Of course, in the natural model, babies learn, from day one, a few, highly effective CCAOs, drawing on their own creative resources to communicate: 'GIVE ME FOOD!' or 'PICK ME UP AND HUG ME!' But all of the cognitive and physical performances which will later enable them to be people who able literally to utter, 'I say, may I have a drink please?' are learnt over several years in many thousands of rehearsals and practices during mostly, essentially, phatic communication expe-riences. Within Intensive Interaction practice, there is likely to be a part of the teacher person's consciousness of course, that is working with a blend of intuition and some conscious guidance. She or he may often even be operating conscious technical awarenesses of the principles of 'interactiveness' in the teaching style they are employing at that moment. These awarenesses may guide tactical moments. Overall, however, if things are working optimally, the teacher too should be experiencing a sort of gentle communicative rapture, completely akin to the sensations visible for Ellen and her friends.

I find this to be one of those wonderful, literally beautiful scientific (apparent) paradoxes; the most important objectives and outcomes for a person – the abilities to communicate in all ways, including BFs and CCAOs – are actually mostly learnt within a long series of essentially phatic experiences. We here in this volume aspire to this absolutely fascinating reality continuing to permeate working practices in our field.

Note

1 In all such studies I have read, the term 'non-conscious' is used, not 'subconscious'. I believe it is felt that use of 'subconscious' is so embedded in the work of psychoanalysts, that there would be a confusion.

Acknowledgements

Thanks and appreciation to Graham Firth, Ian Harris, Lynette Menzies, Julia Rhodes, Gunter Senft, Ben Smith and Lydia Swinton for their helpful discussions with me during the preparation of this chapter. It felt like BFs, but really they were CCAOs.

Thanks also to Ellen and the NCYPE Coordinator Team for the blind frogs.

References

Adler, R.B. and Rodman, G. (2006) *Understanding Human Communication.* New York: Oxford University Press.

Antaki, C., Finlay, W.M.L. and Walton, C. (2007) 'Conversational shaping: staff members solicitation of talk from people with an intellectual impairment', *Qualitative Health Research*, 17(10): 1403–14.

Baumeister, R.F., Zhang, L. and Vohs, K.D. (2004) 'Gossip as cultural learning', *Review of General Psychology*, 8(2): 111–21.

Bradshaw, J. (2001a) 'Complexity of staff communication and reported level of understanding skills in adults with intellectual disability', *Journal of Intellectual Disability Research*, 45(3): 233–43.

Bradshaw, J. (2001b) 'Communication partnerships with people with profound and multiple learning disabilities', *Tizard Learning Disability Review*, 6(2): 6–15.

Burnard, P. (2003) 'Ordinary chat and therapeutic conversation: phatic communication and mental health nursing', *Journal of Psychiatric and Mental Health Nursing*, 10: 678–82.

Burton, G. and Dimbleby, R. (1995) *Between Ourselves: An Introduction to Interpersonal Communication*, 2nd edn. London: Arnold.

Dijksterhuis, A. and Nordgren, L.F. (2006) 'A theory of unconscious thought', *Perspectives on Psychological Science*, 1(2): 95–109.

Dunbar, R. (1996) *Grooming, Gossip and the Evolution of Language*. London: Faber and Faber.

Dunbar, R. (1998) 'Theory of mind and the evolution of language', in J.R. Hurford, M. Studdert-Kennedy and C. Knight (eds), *Approaches to the Evolution of Language*. Cambridge: Cambridge University Press.

Emler, N. (1992) 'The truth about gossip', *Social Psychology Newsletter*, 27: 23–37.

Goleman, D. (2006) *Social Intelligence: The New Science of Human Relationships*. London: Hutchinson.

Harris, J. (1994) 'Language, communication and personal power: a developmental perspective', in J. Coupe O'Kane and B. Smith (eds), *Taking Control: Enabling People with Learning Difficulties*. London: David Fulton.

Hewett, D. and Nind, M. (eds) (1998) *Interaction in Action: Reflections on the Use of Intensive Interaction*. London: David Fulton.

Kelly, R. (2009) 'Twitter study – August 2009', www.pearanalytics.com (accessed January 2011).

Koski, K., Martikainen, K., Burakoff, K. and Launonen, K. (2010) 'Staff members' understandings about communication with individuals who have multiple learning disabilities: a case of Finnish OIVA communication training', *Journal of Intellectual & Developmental Disability*, 35(4): 279–89.

Lakin, J.L. (2006) 'Automatic cognitive processes and nonverbal communication', in V. Manusov and M.L. Patterson (eds), *The Sage Handbook of Nonverbal Communication*. Thousand Oaks, CA: Sage.

Malinowski, B. (1923) 'The problem of meaning in primitive languages', in K.C. Ogden and I.A. Richards (eds), *The Meaning of Meaning. A Study of the Influence of Language upon Thought and of the Science of Symbolism. Supplement 1*. London: Kegan Paul, Trench, Trubner. (Fourth edition revised 1936.)

Markova, J.L., Jahoda, A., Cattermole, M. and Woodward, D. (1992) 'Living in hospital and hostel: the pattern of interactions of people with learning difficulties', *Journal of Intellectual Disability Research*, 36(2): 115–27.

Martikainen, K. and Roisko, E. (2004) 'Interactive skills of personnel and communication partners with intellectual disability', 11th Biennial Conference of the

International Society for Augmentative and Alternative Communication Proceedings, Natal, Brazil.

McAndrew, F.T. (2008) 'Can gossip be good?', *Scientific American Mind*, 19: 26–33.

McConkey, R., Morris, I. and Purcell, M. (1999) 'Communications between staff and adults with intellectual disabilities in naturally occurring settings', *Journal of Intellectual Disability Research*, 43(3): 194–205.

Nind, M. and Hewett, D. (1994) *Access to Communication: Developing the Basics of Communication with People with Severe Learning Difficulties through Intensive Interaction.* London: David Fulton.

Pearce, B.W. (1989) *Communication and the Human Condition.* Chicago, IL: Southern Illinois University Press.

Princeton University (2006) WordNet: http://wordnet.princeton.edu/ (accessed January 2011).

Rutter, M. (1972) *Maternal Deprivation Reassessed.* Harmondsworth: Penguin.

Rutter, M. and Rutter, M. (1993) *Developing Minds: Challenge and Continuity Across the Life Span.* Harmondsworth: Penguin.

Senft, G. (2009) 'Phatic communion', in G. Senft, J.-O. Östman and J. Verschueren (eds), *Culture and Language Use.* Amsterdam: John Benjamins.

Ware, J. (1996) *Creating a Responsive Environment for People with Profound and Multiple Learning Difficulties.* London: David Fulton.

Zilber, D., Shaddock, A., Dowse, L., Rawlings, M., Guggenheimer, S. and Browne, F. (1994) 'Communication patterns in services for people with severe intellectual disabilities: function, form and responsiveness', *Australian Journal of Human Communication Disorders*, 22: 85–98.

Intensive Interaction, emotional development and emotional well-being

Melanie Nind

Chapter overview: why focus on emotion?

Emotion was not at the forefront of our thinking when as teachers at Harperbury Hospital school in the 1980s we started experimenting with what is now widely familiar as Intensive Interaction. It was human connectedness with our students that we sought and local psychologist Geraint Ephraim pointed us to augmented mothering, which led us to research on early caregiver–infant interaction and to the beginnings of communication and social development. Studies from developmental psychology illustrated the power of particular styles of interaction for the development of relationships and individuals, yet little was said about emotion in our discussions about the practice we were developing based on this. We knew that our students, largely cut off from the pleasures of human interaction were far from happy. We knew that some of them had diagnosable mental illness and many more experienced ill-defined poor mental health. In seeking human connectedness we were seeking better emotional well-being for our students – we just did not think about it in those terms then.

In this chapter I address this early void by making explicit the relationship between Intensive Interaction, emotional development and emotional well-being. I will do this by examining some of the theory related to each. The theoretical landscape has changed considerably in the three decades since the early work on Intensive Interaction. The emotional dimension of learning has gained public attention in part owing to Goleman (1996) popularising the concept of emotional intelligence. Weare's (2004) work on emotional literacy has been influential and there is now universal roll-out across England of Social and Emotional Aspects of Learning (SEAL) programmes as part of a national strategy, spreading into secondary education from primary and into the home with Family SEAL. Leaning and Watson (2006) have used Intensive Interaction with the clear intention to develop emotional literacy skills. In the USA the Collaborative for Academic, Social and Emotional Learning (CASEL, 2003) has been active in promoting carefully evaluated interventions, and in Australia whole-school, whole-community approaches have become widespread (Stewart et al., 2004); some of their programmes are being adapted in Europe (Weare and Nind, 2010). There is, though, some dissent regarding this trend, voiced particularly by Ecclestone (2004), as I later discuss. This chapter is therefore timely in addressing the emotional aspects of Intensive Interaction.

Defining emotion

Defining emotion depends on one's theoretical orientation. In understanding emotion in relation to Intensive Interaction, I adopt the view that emotions are 'a crucial and integral component of self development' (Garvey and Fogel, 2007: 51). Emotions, from this dynamic systems perspective, do not exist 'out there' or 'in here', but emerge in the interactions between children and their social sur-roundings. Garvey and Fogel (2007: 51) use the work of Wallon (1984) to explain: 'it is through emotionally charged exchanges with others that children simultaneously experience a sense of connec-tion with and separation from others, thereby contributing to their self development. Children's emotions are not just adaptive reac-tions to situations; instead, the foremost function of emotions is that of communication between self and others ...'.

Unlike in earlier theoretical stances whereby emotions were regarded as internal, discrete states evident through facial expressions, in the newer theoretical work 'emotions are alive experiences dynamically lived and developed over time through co-regulated dialogues with others' (Garvey and Fogel, 2007: 57). Seeing emotion as embedded in the interactive space in this way helps to explain how intertwined the emotional, social and communicative essentially are. It may also explain how emotional development could have remained implicit in Intensive Interaction work, unconsciously yet actively fostered.

Defining emotional well-being

Defining emotional well-being takes us to a different body of work within health promotion and health education in which emotional well-being, linked with mental health, concerns 'the ability to grow and develop, to make relationships and to be resilient in the face of difficulties' (Nind, 2009: 63). Moreover, emotional well-being is: 'A holistic, subjective state which is present when a range of feelings, among them energy, confidence, openness, enjoyment, happiness, calm, and caring are combined and balanced' (Stewart-Brown, 2000: 32). The presence of emotional well-being depends on emotional competence (sometimes referred to as emotional literacy) and engagement in emotional processes (emotional intelligence). Experiencing emotional well-being can come from feeling 'uniquely known, recognized, nurtured and valued' (Weare, 2004: 25). Thus, fostering emotional well-being involves fostering emotional pleasure, satisfaction, relaxation, fun, joy, ability to lose oneself in the moment, and to experience engagement or inner peace.

Emotional well-being is increasingly understood as fundamentally connected with the ability to learn in a symbiotic process. Teachers have often worked on the premise that we learn better when we feel good and that we feel good when we are learning, thus creating a virtuous cycle. This is now also supported by cognitive neuroscience (see, for example, Damasio, 2000; LeDoux, 1998). Furthermore, emotional well-being is understood to make a difference to the person at the time, and to their long-term development; it is this latter that is influencing governments to emphasise emotional literacy in their education policy and guidance.

Theories of emotional development in infancy

I turn now to a theoretical exploration of how emotions develop in infancy, primarily using developmental psychology studies of the impact of caregiver–infant interaction. This is significant for, as Zeedyk (2006: 323) argues, 'intense emotional engagement between mothers and infants is regarded as the best foundation for later development'. In discussing this research I draw out the relevance for Intensive Interaction and the importance for well-being. I begin with dynamic systems theory as advocated by Thelen (1989).

Dynamic systems theory

A central premise of dynamic systems theory is that 'systems can generate novelty through their own activity' (Smith and Thelen, 2003: 343); thereby, 'In human development, every neural event, every reach, every smile and every social encounter sets the stage for the next and the real-time causal force behind change' (ibid.: 347). A dynamic systems approach moves beyond studying emotions as discrete states expressed outwardly through the face (for example, Izard, 1997) to studying how the different elements of communication (face, gaze, body, vocalisations, gestures) 'coalesce into coherent emotion patterns that support infants' meaningful relationships with others' (Garvey and Fogel, 2008: 62).

Camras and Witherington (2005) review the ways in which theories of emotional development have themselves developed. Important in this development is Garvey and Fogel's (2008: 63) contention that emotions emerge through communication and 'help punctuate the dynamic flow of communication by opening (or closing) opportunities for individuals to experience themselves in relation to others'. Thus, emotions are dynamic aspects of encounters and development. Garvey and Fogel describe a series of mother–infant interactions in which:

> these two individuals may co-create a positively meaningful relationship characterized by a pleasant inclination toward one another, a desire to be together, a feeling of benefit and joy in the presence of the other. This positive emotional inclination in turn facilitates the participants' future engagement in mutually gratifying and creative experiences. (Garvey and Fogel, 2008: 64)

This sense of well-being is absolutely what Intensive Interaction attempts to recreate with our emphasis on making 'every interaction a mutually enjoyable and satisfying experience' (Nind and Hewett, 2005: 14).

Emotional development comes from the process of co-regulation in which the caregiver and infant focus on each other and affect the interaction between them. Their emotional orientation may converge as they respond to and amplify each other's contribution to the interactive flow, building the relationship, and diverge enabling the infant to see him/herself as separate (Garvey and Fogel, 2007). In this way emotions are essential to infants' self development and to simultaneously fostering 'a sense of connection with and differentiation from others' (Garvey and Fogel, 2007: 72).

The development of emotions also encompasses development of an emotional repertoire and the infant is an active agent in this. Garvey and Fogel (2007: 51) give the following example: 'when playing with and smiling at their mothers, infants do not merely respond to their mothers; instead infants actively contribute to the feelings of joy as they participate in an episode of positive emotional communication with their mothers'. Thus, as infants learn about being – being happy, being excited and so on – this is 'being-in-relation' to others (Garvey and Fogel, 2007: 73), which is fundamental in the building of relationships. This sense of reciprocal, mutual enjoyment of each other will be very familiar to Intensive Interaction practitioners as the bedrock of what we set out to achieve in interactive episodes. What we may be less conscious of is the development of an emotional repertoire alongside the development of a repertoire of familiar interactive games.

Contingent responding and feedback

From a different theoretical standpoint of a social-biofeedback model, Gergely and Watson (1999: 102) focus on the process by which infants become aware of their emotional dispositions through 'social mirroring'. They contend that for infants becoming aware of their internal affective states being able to detect contingency is crucial as is caregivers' contingent reflections of infants' emotions. Again, contingent responding is a core principle of Intensive Interaction, adopted because of awareness of its importance in caregiver–infant interaction.

Some researchers, such as Meltzoff and Gopnik (1993), argue infants have emotional awareness from birth, based on evidence of neonatal imitation (Meltzoff and Moore, 1989). One line of argument is that, by imitating the caregiver's facial expression of emotion, pre-wired connections in the infant are activated, triggering the infant to feel the corresponding physiological emotion (see Ekman et al., 1983). Critical of this view, Gergely and Watson (1999: 112) review recent empirical research into early caregiver–infant interactions (for example, Hains and Muir, 1996; Kaye, 1982; Murray and Trevarthen, 1985; Papousek and Papousek, 1989; Sroufe, 1996; Stern, 1985; Tronick, 1989), which has largely 'confirmed the traditional view that *facial and vocal mirroring of affective behavior* may be a central feature of parental affect-regulative interactions during the first year' (original italics). They reflect on the dominant biosocial view of emotional development in which mother and infant are understood to form an affective communication system from their first interactions (see, for example, Beebe et al., 1992; Bowlby, 1969; Brazelton et al., 1974; Hobson, 1993) with the mother modulating the infant's affective states before the infant develops mechanisms to do so. It has been shown that caregivers often sensitively attune their affective responses to modulate infants' emotional states (Tronick, 1989), unless caregivers themselves are depressed (Murray et al., 1996; Tronick, 1989; Tronick and Field, 1986) when contingent affective interactions decrease.

Gergely and Watson (1999: 113) argue that 'whereas theoretical, clinical, and empirical approaches all converge on the view that parental affect-reflective interactions play a central role in early emotional and self-development, the exact nature of the causal mechanisms mediating such effects has not yet been identified'. They point to the temporal, sensory relational, and spatial elements of contingency and their combined importance. Intensive Interaction uses deliberate contingent responding to create feelings of effectiveness necessary to the desire to explore the environment and the emotional literacy of the person with learning difficulties. Imitation is a fine example of contingent responding with infants and people with learning difficulties, and Zeedyk (2006: 331) places particular value on imitation, for its power in creating emotional intimacy: 'imitation provides the closest correspondence between self and other'.

In Intensive Interaction we are conscious that imitation is not accurate, more like modified reflecting (Nind and Hewett, 2005: 119). The potential importance of this is highlighted by Gergely and Watson (1999) in their exploration of why, when caregivers mirror the negative affective state their infant is displaying, this is not read by the infant as the caregiver's own affective state. This could result in the negative affect escalating rather than becoming regulated in the infant. This is averted, they argue, by the process in which caregivers' affect-reflective emotion displays are 'marked' to make them perceptibly different from real expressions of emotion, by being '*an exaggerated version* of the parent's realistic emotion expression' (ibid.: 117, original emphasis). Gergely and Watson hypothesise that this marking allows the infant 'to referentially anchor the marked mirroring stimulus as expressing his or her *own* self-state' (1999: 117). It is these marked emotional displays that are likely to be contingent on the infant and that show the importance of contingent responding for developing emotional awareness.

Touch

The role of facial expression in emotional development is frequently highlighted, yet there is also a body of work on the importance of touch that has been influential on Intensive Interaction. Montagu (1986, 1995) has shown how touch is fundamental to health, well-being and cognitive development. Touch provides a direct and understandable form of contact between infants and caregivers and a fundamental experience in the development of communication powers. Touch also has a deep emotional and psychological significance as an aspect of non-verbal interacting; it is one of the underpinning experiences to all areas of human development, a primary means for providing comfort and for communicating empathy and contributes to the emotional intimacy stressed by Zeedyk (2006).

Understanding of the potential value of touch for emotional well-being has led to a host of touch-based interventions which I have discussed previously (Nind, 2009). These include massage therapy which has been linked with weight gain in pre-term babies (Scafidi et al., 1996), improved sociability of babies of depressed mothers (Field et al., 1996), and better attentiveness among children with autism (Field et al., 1997). In these interventions though, the touch is 'technical' instead of 'natural' (Piper and Smith, 2003). In Intensive Interaction touch is used as part of a natural process of interaction and has stronger echoes of the touch used naturally by caregiver as part of the language of relationship building (see Hewett, 2007, for a fuller discussion).

Attachment theory

The attachment theory of Bowlby (1969) focuses in the psychological construct of attachments: the bonds that form between primary caregivers and infants. These attachments are part of an attachment system which becomes the context for subsequent transactions with the social environment, particularly social relationships (Sroufe, 1988). Attachment experiences are hypothesised to impact on the individual's later relationships (Golding, 2008) and so impact on well-being. This happens through the formation of internal working models based on early caregiving and care-seeking interactions. These internal working models 'incorporate the capacity for self-regulation, the ability to identify and reflect on internal states of self and others, mental representations of self and others, and strategies for managing relationship experiences based on those mental representations' (Atwool, 2006: 318). But it is attachment that balances the infant's need for a secure base – a relational place of safety – with the need for exploration or challenge (Bowlby, 1977). As Weare (2004: 42) argues, emotional and social development based on attachment is 'the basis for forming connections with others, the basis on which all social competences are based'.

In Intensive Interaction we have been conscious of the ways in which the types of interactions we promote and engage in, by their very nature, create a sense of attachment and bonding. This echoes leading accounts of infant intersubjectivity which recognise the importance of bonding (Zeedyk, 2006). Theoretically grounded practical help with forming attachments is extremely helpful for parents using the approach as they have reported being enabled to feel newly connected to their children. Parents of one son with autism using Intensive Interaction explain:

> My son grins broadly and chuckles, puts his arms around my neck, looks deep into my eyes, and for a moment we share a precious moment of shared happiness ... We are seeing more and more of Gary's feelings, and a greater variety of them too, but more important and what is absolutely fundamental to our approach with Gary, is the sharing of emotions. This brings him in as a part of our family, and makes him one of us. It wasn't always like this. (Taylor and Taylor, 1998: 209)

For professionals, however, this has meant the need to balance getting involved and attached at some level with putting in place measures to support the person, bearing in mind this is not an exclusive parenting-type relationship. For the person with learning difficulties a team approach and attachments with more than one interactive partner are important to prevent potential isolation and hurt. For the Intensive Interaction practitioner a team approach is necessary to enable a safe space to talk about their emotional attachments and how they will be managed.

Theories of emotional well-being and how it can be supported

I have shown how, according to a selection of theories, emotional development proceeds in infancy and drawn some connections between these processes, processes of Intensive Interaction and the emergence of social and emotional well-being. I now turn to different bodies of literature on well-being itself. I discuss first the well-being (or rather lack of it) of people with learning difficulties before addressing the literature on how well-being is best promoted.

Emotional well-being in people with learning difficulties

Emotional well-being is closely bound up with quality of life (Moss et al., 2000) with the same environmental factors associated with each: receiving individually tailored support to become full participants in the life of the community, developing skills and independence, being given appropriate choices and control over one's life, and being treated with respect in a safe and secure environment (Emerson et al., 1996). Historically these factors have been lacking for people with learning difficulties who have unsurprisingly not always enjoyed good quality of life or well-being. Indeed, it is only in the 1990s and 2000s that the emotional lives of people with learning difficulties have attracted the attention of researchers (Moss et al., 2000). Arthur (2003: 25) argues that the emotional lives of people with learning disabilities were 'submerged by the behavioural technologies of the 1970s and 1980s'. The move to deinstitutionalisation has partly been about a better quality of life but, as Arthur (2003) argues, change of physical environment is pointless if life is characterised by loneliness, isolation, fear and apathy, if social interactions remain limited, if there is little concern for the subjective quality of the individual's experience, and if independent living skills and the treatment of challenging behaviour are prioritised over emotional well-being.

The poor emotional well-being of people with learning difficulties has been exposed in research about mental health in which people with learning difficulties have been shown to be more likely to experience mental health difficulties during their lives than the general population (Emerson, 2003), with mental health difficulties increasing in proportion to the severity of multiple disabilities (Sinason, 1994). As Hatton (2002) notes, however, less is known about the mental health of people with more severe difficulties/disabilities. There is research evidence though, that people with profound learning difficulties experience stressful emotions even when overt signs may be absent (Chaney, 1996). The *Count Us In* inquiry into meeting the mental health needs of young people (Foundation for People with Learning Disabilities, 2002) included among the recommendations for addressing environmental factors in supporting the resilience of people with learning difficulties, finding ways to communicate that can enhance a sense of well-being and promote control. Relationships and emotions have become a priority of policy-makers (for example, DoH, 2001: objective 7).

Meaningful relationships and the ability to take action in an environment that is contingent and responsive, which is intrinsic to Intensive Interaction, is argued to be essential for emotional well-being in people with learning difficulties (Harris, 1994) as well as infants (Orley, 1996). People with learning difficulties themselves support this and it is in keeping with a social model of mental distress (Williams and Heslop, 2005). The practical process of this in

Intensive Interaction involves practitioners in attuning to their communication partner's state of arousal, tempo, modal preferences *and* emotional state. The outcome of the whole package of processes includes better emotional well-being. The evidence for this lies in published personal testimony (for example, Taylor and Taylor, 1998), explorations of its use (for example, Davies et al., 2008) and efficacy studies (for example, Kellett, 2005).

Educational/inter-agency approaches to promoting emotional well-being

Outside of the field of learning difficulties considerable research is being invested into an understanding of what works in promoting well-being (or mental health) in families, schools, work places and so on (Weare and Nind, in press). The outcome is evidence that holistic approaches are particularly effective (Wells et al., 2003). There has been a shift in emphasis from looking at individual problems and solutions, to looking at environments, interactions between people and between factors, and at 'positive capacities rather than problems and deficits' (Weare, 2004: 53). This has led to a stress on proactive, preventative work concerned with the whole person and their environment of which Intensive Interaction, as I have argued elsewhere (Nind, 2009), is a prime example.

Evidence of the benefits of a holistic approach has also pointed to the need for an embedded, coherent, congruent approach across the whole organisation. This suggests that a culture of Intensive Interaction would be more potent than Intensive Interaction practice among incongruent practices, and there is evidence to support this (Kellett and Nind, 2003). Proponents of well-being/mental health promotion advocate social contexts that foster productive, pleasant relationships, teamwork, mutual responsibility and delight in the company of others. This requires a long-term, developmental approach involving the whole community taking care of staff as well as students'/clients' well-being; 'the more there are in a community who are socially and emotionally competent the easier it is to support those with acute problems' (Nind, 2009: 66). Thus, healthy environments are those where emotions are accepted as normal and unthreatening, discussed freely, expressed in safe ways, written about in policies, and considered in decision-making (Weare, 2004). In these environments Intensive Interaction can flourish as staff are less stressed and not overwhelmed by the feelings that the behaviours of people with learning difficulties can elicit in them, and in another virtuous cycle, by enabling positive interactions and positive emotions Intensive Interaction can help to create these emotionally healthy environments. At its best this becomes self-sustaining in a self-regulating system of the kind described in dynamic systems theory.

Weare (2004), in identifying the underpinning principles of effective emotional literacy programmes and approaches, points to the necessity for them to be sustainable, explicit, developmentally appropriate with clear goals and clear roles. Again, Intensive Interaction is a good example of these principles in action. The generation of mutually satisfying interactions is central to its sustainability. Focusing on where the person is at developmentally, rather than where normatively they should be, is what liberates the practitioner to achieve a good interactive fit. Understanding that the goal is to enjoy the process, enjoy the person and have the best possible interaction, rather than perform some task or achieve a target, provides the practitioner with a very clear goal and role. The interactions are designed to introduce the person with learning difficulties to the social world, to attending to faces and voices, getting feedback and making things happen, helping them feel 'uniquely known, recognized, nurtured and valued' (Weare, 2004: 25).

The relationship between Intensive Interaction and emotional well-being can be understood in more simple terms, however, stemming from the establishment of the interactions themselves. Mutual pleasure in the interactions helps the interactive partners to feel relaxed and secure – to lose themselves in the interaction. It motivates both partners to want to repeat the experience and so sustains an ongoing process of communicative, cognitive, social and emotional engagement. Thus, the person with learning difficulties is enabled to achieve states of self-experience (joy, suspense, excitement) as Stern (1985) describes happens in infants.

Intensive Interaction as a 'therapeutic' intervention

Intensive Interaction is sometimes referred to as a therapeutic intervention (for example, Caldwell, 2006; Leaning and Watson, 2006). This may reflect, as some sociologists argue, that therapeutic ideas are pervasive in what has become a 'therapeutic society' (Pilgrim and Rogers, 1999). Writing about education, Norwich and Lewis (2005: 11) use the phrase 'the uncertain interface between teaching and therapeutic interventions that are learning based' to describe programmes outside ordinary curriculum planning that are designed to address the difficulties of specific learners. This could describe Intensive Interaction in some contexts, while in others Intensive Interaction is clearly educational and at the very heart of the curriculum and curriculum planning process. On a continuum from behavioural to therapeutic, however, we have argued (Nind and Hewett 2005: 13) that Intensive Interaction, as 'a gentle way of facilitating development', would fit better with more therapeutic approaches. Frankish and Terry (2003: 8) advocate emotional development therapies for the 'the most disturbed group [of people with learning disabilities, who are] often self-harming and assaultative with a full range of anti-social behaviours and unresponsive to human contact'. Such therapies provide an environment suited to a child's stage of emotional development and Intensive Interaction partially fits this requirement, though the focus is more holistic and not explicitly psychodynamic.

Increasingly, as Intensive Interaction has been adopted more widely by families, carers, speech and language therapists, play therapists, and so on, the purposes of Intensive Interaction beyond the educational have been consolidated. Whether Intensive Interaction is seen as educational or not, it is usually seen as developmental, though for some users of Intensive Interaction it is just about providing better quality of care. Firth has helped to clarify this with his dual aspect process model of Intensive Interaction distinguishing between the 'social inclusion process model', in which practitioners aim to respond to the communication of people with learning difficulties as part of a social inclusion agenda, and the 'developmental process model', in which they have identifiably educative or developmental goals. These nuanced understandings of the benefits in the moment, together with the benefits in the long term, may make the question of whether Intensive Interaction is therapeutic redundant, but discussion of emotional development and emotional well-being nevertheless foregrounds the therapeutic.

Ecclestone (2004) has led the backlash against the emphasis on well-being with a critique of the work on the social and emotional aspects of learning in schools, seeing the language of learners being 'at-risk', 'vulnerable', 'hard to reach', and so on, and the support for emotional well-being that comes with it as hugely problematic. She questions these developments and their underlying assumptions that more people are emotionally fragile because of the ways in which they recast teachers and learners and prioritise the emotional aspects of learning over academic learning. Ecclestone does not have people with learning difficulties in mind in these arguments, but she does juxtapose nurturing and teaching and places academic needs and emotional well-being in a mutually exclusive relationship. This does not concur with the theories and arguments in this chapter.

☐ Summary

Intensive Interaction is a helpful, holistic approach in the interests of the mental health or emotional states of people with the most severe learning difficulties. In this population, who have been lacking approaches sensitive to their emotional needs, Intensive Interaction is a practical route into understanding how an individual with idiosyncratic, perhaps pre-intentional communication is feeling. Using Intensive Interaction enables practitioners to read and interpret such communications, to have insights into changes of behaviours and states and into their well-being. In keeping with emotional literacy programmes Intensive Interaction works on the premise that behaviour has meaning and emotional origins. Working in mutually supportive teams practitioners help to sustain interactions, feelings of efficacy, and thereby well-being for the parties involved.

References

Arthur, A.R. (2003) 'The emotional lives of people with learning disability', *British Journal of Learning Disabilities.* 31: 25–30.

Atwool, N. (2006) 'Attachment and resilience: Implications for children in care', *Child Care in Practice*, 12(4): 315–30.

Beebe, B., Jaffe, J. and Lachmann, F.M. (1992) 'A dyadic systems view of communication', in N. Skolnick and S. Warshaw (eds), *Relational Perspectives in Psychoanalysis*. Hillsdale, NJ: Analytic Press.

Bowlby, J. (1969) *Attachment and Loss: Vol. 1. Attachment.* New York: Basic Books.

Bowlby, J. (1977) 'The making and breaking of attachment bonds: II. Some principles of psychotherapy', *British Journal of Psychiatry*, 130: 421–31.

Brazelton, T.B., Koslowski, B. and Main, M. (1974) 'The origins of reciprocity: the early mother–infant interaction', in M. Lewis and L.A. Rosenblum (eds), *The Effect of the Infant on its Caregiver*. New York: Wiley.

Caldwell, P. (2006) 'Speaking the other's language: imitation as a gateway to relationship', *Infant and Child Development*, 15(3): 275–82.

Camras, L.A. and Witherington, D.C. (2005) 'Dynamical systems approaches to emotional development', *Developmental Review*, 25(3–4): 328–50.

Chaney, R.H. (1996) 'Psychological stress in people with profound mental retardation', *Journal of Intellectual Disability Research*, 40(4): 305–10.

Collaborative for Academic, Social and Emotional Learning (CASEL) (2003) *Safe and Sound, Programme Descriptions*: www.casel.org/pub/safeandsound.php (accessed 12 February 2010).

Damasio, A. (2000) *The Feeling of What Happens*. London: Vintage.

Davies, C.E., Zeedyk, M.S., Wall, S., Betts, N. and Parry, S. (2008) 'Intensive

Interaction increases engagement in Romanian children with a history of severe neglect and communication impairment', in M.S. Zeedyk (ed.), *Making Contact: Promoting Social Interaction for Individuals with Communication Impairments*. London: Jessica Kingsley.

Department of Health (DoH) (2001) *Valuing People: A Strategy for Learning Disability for the 21st Century*. London: Department of Health.

Ecclestone, K. (2004) 'Learning or therapy? The demoralisation of education', *British Journal of Educational Studies*, 52(2): 112–37.

Ekman, P., Levenson, R.W. and Friesen, W.V. (1983) 'Autonomic nervous system activity distinguishes between emotions', *Science*, 221: 1208–10.

Emerson, E. (2003) 'The prevalence of psychiatric disorders in children and adolescents with and without intellectual disabilities', *Journal of Intellectual Disability Research*, 47: 51–8.

Emerson, E., Cullen, C., Hatton, C. and Cross, B. (1996) *Residential Provision for People with Learning Disabilities: Summary Report*. Manchester: Hester Adrian Research Centre.

Field, T., Grizzle, N., Scafidi, F., Abrams, S., Richardson, S., Kuhn, C. and Shanberg, S. (1996) 'Massage therapy for infants of depressed mothers', *Infant Behavior and Development*, 19: 109–14.

Field, T., Lasko, D., Mundy, P., Henteleff, T., Talpins, S. and Dowling, M. (1997) 'Autistic children's attentiveness and responsivity improve after touch therapy', *Journal of Autism and Developmental Disorders*, 27: 333–8.

Foundation for People with Learning Disabilities (2002) *Count Us In. The Report of the Committee of Inquiry into Meeting the Mental Health Needs of Young People with Learning Disabilities*. London: Mental Health Foundation.

Frankish, P. and Terry, S. (2003) 'Modern therapeutic approaches in learning disability services', *Tizard Learning Disability Review*, 8(3): 3–10.

Garvey, A. and Fogel, A. (2007) 'Dialogical change processes, emotions, and the early emergence of self', *International Journal for Dialogical Science*, 2(1): 51–76.

Garvey, A. and Fogel, A. (2008) 'Emotions and communication as a dynamic developmental system', *Espaciotiempo*, 2: 62–73.

Gergely, G. and Watson, J.S. (1999) 'Early socio-emotional development: contingency perception and the social-biofeedback model', in P. Rochat (ed.), *Early Social Cognition: Understanding Others in the First Months of Life*. Mahwah, NJ: Lawrence Erlbaum.

Golding, K.S. (2008) *Nurturing Attachments: Supporting Children Who Are Fostered or Adopted*. London: Jessica Kingsley.

Goleman, D. (1996) *Emotional Intelligence*. London: Bloomsbury.

Hains, S.M.J. and Muir, D.W. (1996) 'Infant sensitivity to adult eye direction', *Child Development*, 67: 1940–51.

Harris, J. (1994) 'Language, communication and personal power: a developmental perspective', in J. Coupe O'Kane and B. Smith (eds), *Taking Control: Enabling People with Learning Difficulties*. London: David Fulton.

Hatton, C. (2002) 'Psychosocial interventions for adults with intellectual disabilities and mental health problems: a review', *Journal of Mental Health*, 11(4): 357–73.

Hewett, D. (2007) 'Do touch: physical contact and people who have severe, profound and multiple learning difficulties', *Support for Learning*, 22(3): 116–23.

Hobson, R.P. (1993) *Autism and the Development of Mind*. Hove: Lawrence Erlbaum.

Izard, C.E. (1997) 'Emotions and facial expressions: a perspective from differential emotions theory', in J.A. Russel and J.M. Fernandez-Dols (eds), *The Psychology of Facial Expression*. New York: Cambridge University Press.

Kaye, S. (1982) 'Psychoanalytic perspectives on learning disability', *Journal of Contemporary Psychotherapy*, 13: 83–93.

Kellett, M. (2005) Catherine's legacy: social communication development for individuals with profound learning difficulties and fragile life expectancies', *British Journal of Special Education*, 32(3): 116–21.

Kellett, M. and Nind, M. (2003) *Implementing Intensive Interaction in Schools: Guidance for Practitioners, Managers and Coordinators*. London: David Fulton.

Leaning, B. and Watson, T. (2006) 'From the inside looking out – an Intensive Interaction group for people with profound and multiple learning disabilities', *British Journal of Learning Disabilities*, 34(2): 103–9.

LeDoux, J. (1998) *The Emotional Brain*. London: Phoenix.

Meltzoff, A.N. and Gopnik, A. (1993) 'The role of imitation in understanding persons and developing a theory of mind', in S. Baron-Cohen, H. Tager-Flusberg and D.J. Cohen (eds), *Understanding Other Minds: Perspectives from Autism*. Oxford: Oxford University Press.

Meltzoff, A.N. and Moore, M.K. (1989) 'Imitation in newborn infants: exploring the range of gestures imitated and the underlying mechanisms', *Developmental Psychology*, 25: 954–62.

Montagu, A. (1986) *Touching: The Human Significance of the Skin*. New York: Columbia.

Montagu, A. (1995) 'Animadversions on the development of a theory of touch', in T. Field (ed.), *Touch in Early Development*. Hillsdale, NJ: Lawrence Erlbaum.

Moss, S., Bouras, N. and Holt, G. (2000) 'Mental health services for people with intellectual disability: a conceptual framework', *Journal of Intellectual Disability Research*, 44(2): 97–107.

Murray, L. and Trevarthen, C. (1985) 'Emotional regulation of interactions between two-month-olds and their mothers', in T.M. Field and N.A. Fox (eds). *Social Perception in Infants*. Norwood, NJ: Ablex.

Murray, L., Fiori-Cowley, A., Hooper, R. and Cooper, P. (1996) 'The impact of postnatal depression and associated adversity on early mother–infant interactions and later infant outcomes', *Child Development*, 67: 2512–26.

Nind, M. (2009) 'Promoting the emotional well-being of people with profound and multiple learning disabilities: a holistic approach through Intensive Interaction', in G. Pawlyn and S. Carnaby (eds), *Profound and Multiple Learning*

Disabilities: Nursing Complex Needs. Oxford: Blackwell.

Nind, M. and Hewett, D. (2005) *Access to Communication: Developing the Basics of Communication with People with Severe Learning Difficulties through Intensive Interaction*, 2nd edn. London: David Fulton.

Norwich, B. and Lewis, A. (2005) 'How specialized is teaching pupils with disabilities and difficulties?', in B. Norwich and A. Lewis (eds), *Special Teaching for Special Children.* Maidenhead: Open University Press.

Orley, J. (1996) 'World Health Organization: programme on mental health', *Journal of Mental Health*, 5(3): 319–22.

Papousek, H. and Papousek, M. (1989) 'Forms and functions of vocal matching in interactions between mothers and their precanonical infants', *First Language*, 9: 137–58.

Pilgrim, D. and Rogers, A. (1999) *A Sociology of Mental Health and Illness*, 2nd edn. Buckingham: Open University Press.

Piper, H. and Smith, H. (2003) 'Touch in educational and child care settings: dilemmas and responses', *British Educational Research Journal*, 29(6): 879–94.

Scafidi, F.A., Field, T.M., Wheeden, A., Schanberg, S., Kuhn, C., Symanski, R., Zimmerman, E. and Bandstra, E.S. (1996) 'Cocaine-exposed preterm neonates show behavioral and hormonal differences', *Pediatrics*, 97: 851–5.

Sinason, V. (1994) *Mental Handicap and the Human Condition.* London: Free Association Books.

Smith, B. and Thelen, E. (2003) 'Development as a dynamic system', *Trends in Cognitive Sciences*, 7(8): 343–8.

Sroufe, L.A. (1988) 'The role of infant–caregiver attachment in development', in J. Belsky and T. Nezworski (eds), *Clinical Implications of Attachment.* Hillsdale, NJ: Lawrence Erlbaum.

Sroufe, L.A. (1996) *Emotional Development: The Organization of Emotional Life in the Early Years.* New York: Cambridge University Press.

Stern, D.N. (1985) *The Interpersonal World of the Infant.* New York: Basic Books.

Stewart, D., Sun, J., Patterson, C., Lemerle, K. and Hardie, M. (2004) 'Promoting and building resilience in primary school communities: evidence from a comprehensive "health promoting school" approach', *International Journal of Mental Health Promotion*, 6(3): 26–33.

Stewart-Brown, S. (2000) 'Parenting, wellbeing, health and disease', in A. Buchanan and B. Hudson (eds), *Promoting Children's Emotional Well-being.* Oxford: Oxford University Press.

Taylor, B. and Taylor, S. (1998) 'Gary's story: parents doing Intensive Interaction', in D. Hewett and M. Nind (eds), *Interaction in Action.* London: David Fulton.

Thelen, E. (1989) 'Self-organization in developmental processes: can systems approaches work', in M.R. Gunnar and E. Thelen (eds), *Minnesota Symposium on Child Psychology. Vol. 22. Systems and Development.* Hillsdale, NJ: Lawrence Erlbaum.

Tronick, E.Z. (1989) 'Emotions and emotional communication in infants', *American Psychologist*, 44: 112–19.

Tronick, E.Z. and Field, T. (1986) *Maternal Depression and Infant Disturbance.* San Francisco, CA: Jossey-Bass.

Wallon, H. (1984) 'The emotions', in G. Voyat (ed.), *The World of Henri Wallon.* New York: Jason Aronson.

Weare, K. (2004) *Developing the Emotionally Literate School.* London: Paul Chapman Publishing.

Weare, K. and Nind, M. (2010) 'Identifying evidence-based work on mental health promotion in schools in Europe: an interim report on the DataPrev project', *Advances in School Mental Health Promotion*, 3(2): 36–44.

Wells, J., Barlow, J. and Stewart-Brown, S. (2003) 'A systematic review of universal approaches to mental health promotion in schools', *Health Education*, 103: 197–204.

Williams, V. and Heslop, P. (2005) 'Mental health support needs of people with a learning difficulty: a medical or a social model?', *Disability & Society*, 20(3): 231–45.

Zeedyk, M.S. (2006) 'From intersubjectivity to subjectivity: the transformative roles of emotional intimacy and imitation', *Infant and Child Development*, 15(3): 321–44.

3

Interactive approaches to teaching and learning

Penny Lacey

Chapter overview

It is the intention, in this chapter, to trace the theoretical background to Intensive Interaction, through the exploration of a wider set of ideas known as interactive approaches to teaching and learning. By broadening the parameters of the inquiry, it is intended to give readers the understanding necessary to be able to think creatively about the teaching and learning associated with the early stages of developing social interaction. The chapter is structured around the attempt to answer the following questions.

- What are interactive approaches to teaching and learning?
- What are the theoretical underpinnings in terms of child development and learning?
- How are these underpinnings put into pedagogical practice?
- What are the roles of the learner and the teacher (or more experienced person) in interactive approaches?
- What do interactive approaches look like for learners with profound disabilities?

To answer these questions several areas of psychology and pedagogy have been examined. Few are directly related to people with profound disabilities but the connections are explicitly made where possible. People at an early stage of understanding social interaction are not expected to be able to engage in dialogic, active or enquiry-based learning as typical learners but the principles that underlie these methods are transferrable in a potentially helpful way.

Interactive approaches to teaching and learning in relation to children and young people with severe learning difficulties developed in the UK in response to the prevailing dominance of behavioural approaches in the 1980s (Foxen and McBrien, 1981). McConkey (1981) questioned the way in which approaches such as the Education of the Developmentally Young (EDY) concentrated on teaching skills in a manner that did not necessarily lead to understanding when, where and how to use those skills. For example, the Distar Language Programme encouraged imitation of phrases on command. The method resulted in pupils learning phrases that they could only produce in that one context. If they did utter them elsewhere, it was rarely with understanding.

In response to McConkey's (1981) article 'Education without understanding?', Smith et al. (1983) showed how 'Education with understanding' could be achieved through the adoption of more interactive approaches to teaching and learning. From these small beginnings, grew a group of practitioners and researchers committed to developing interactive approaches to teaching and learning with children with severe learning difficulties and several met together for a conference at Westhill College in Birmingham in 1987. The proceedings were published in a collection (Smith, 1987) and covered topics such as language (Harris, 1987), early cognition (Glenn, 1987) and curriculum (Hewett and Nind, 1987; Lacey, 1987).

After the 1988 Education Act and the birth of the National Curriculum, a second conference was convened where the participants attempted to show how interactive approaches could be developed through the subjects of the National Curriculum (Smith, 1990). It was extremely hard for the impetus for interactive approaches to continue at this time as both practitioners and researchers were caught up in the struggle, first, to show the relevance of the National Curriculum to children with severe and profound learning difficulties and, later, to embrace the national strategies and the target-driven agenda. Collis and Lacey's (1996) book *Interactive Approaches to Teaching: A Framework for INSET* was one of the few publications to continue to promote interactive approaches in general, showing how assessment, record-keeping, the curriculum and teaching approaches could be influenced by a view of the processes of education rather than by the products. They encouraged the teaching of thinking and problem-solving and the importance of intrinsic rather than extrinsic rewards. Children who learn because they enjoy the learning and feel fully involved are more likely to develop understanding than those who have to be rewarded with food and stickers, especially if they find it hard to figure out why they are being rewarded. Interactive approaches had much to offer and these are now under scrutiny in this chapter.

Interactive approaches and child development

Interactive approaches have their routes in cognitive psychology and a desire to understand the development of such processes as thinking, perceiving, reasoning, judging, problem-solving as well as the development of communication and language. There is no single definition, although a diagram from Collis and Lacey (1996) contains some of the central themes (Figure 3.1). The central circle in Figure 3.1 describes two of the fundamentals of interactive approaches, while the outer circle illustrates the two main themes.

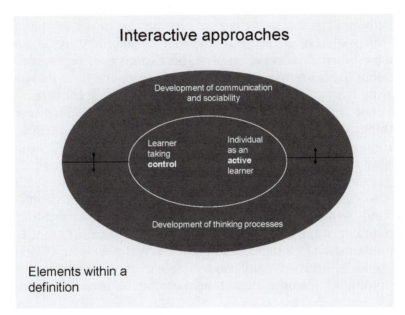

Figure 3.1 Elements within a definition
Source: Collis and Lacey (1996)

The first fundamental refers to children as being active in their learning. They actively modify the information they receive through their senses, not always by being physically active but by actively engaging their minds. Typically developing infants engage physically with objects and people but as they grow and develop they can rely more and more on abstract thought. Actively engaging the mind is vital for the development of understanding and lifts learners from 'learned responses' to 'intelligent behaviour'. This distinction is particularly important when considering the learning of people with profound learning disability as often they develop an automatic response to a stimulus. For example, if they are given an object they will always treat it in the same way perhaps by throwing or mouthing it. Learning to explore that object involves actively engaging the mind by taking in information about shape, size, weight and colour in an attempt to make sense of it. Typical infants develop schema such as squeezing, banging, pulling, nesting by constantly comparing and contrasting information (Doherty and Hughes, 2009). People with profound learning disabilities find this active development of ideas about their world particularly difficult but being an active learner is fundamental to interactive approaches and finding ways of actively engaging people with profound learning disabilities is vital (Collis and Lacey, 1996).

The second fundamental is very closely related to the first as it refers to learners taking control of their own learning. To be active learners, typical infants soon become involved in making things happen and gradually understand that their actions are the causes of the effects they can see, hear or feel. Initially, they accidentally make mobiles move but when this occurs on several occasions they begin to understand that they can make this happen. Experiments have shown that if a string is attached from a typical baby's leg to a mobile, then there is far more leg movement than if there is no connection between the two things. The baby is becoming aware that she or he can control the environment (Goswami, 2008). People with profound learning disability find these connections hard to make and can need a great many examples before contingency awareness is reached (Glenn, 1987). It is vital to set up a responsive environment where people with profound learning disabilities can learn to be in control. If the environment is not responsive then the active learning, that is, the first fundamental in interactive approaches, will not occur. Often what does occur is 'learned helplessness' (Seligman, 1975) where people with profound learning disabilities become so used to having no control that they cease to try.

Once the two fundamentals of being an active learner and taking control over that learning have been established, then development of thinking processes and communication and sociability with others are possible. The learning process begins with sensing because young babies are not yet ready for rational thinking, and this sensing is accompanied by attending, which is deliberate and active and can never be achieved automatically. The quality of the attending determines the quality of perceiving, thinking and memorising (De Witt, 2009). Three components of learning appear to be important especially at this early stage: exploration, imitation and repetition. These are, of course, all part of active learning and enable young children to become increasingly autonomous.

Doherty and Hughes (2009) suggest that although Piaget's theory of development has been criticised in its detail, there are still valid implications for teaching and learning. According to Piaget, children need to be actively engaged in exploring their surroundings, constructing their own understanding through their own senses. They gradually understand concepts that are more and more abstract but, initially, concrete experiences are crucial to very young children. Adults need to provide an environment that encourages development, full of interesting and responsive objects and activities.

Piaget's view of children's learning is often characterised as promoting individual endeavour. The child is viewed as an experimental scientist, developing ideas and concepts through trial and error. A different view is presented by Vygotsky (1987), who argued that children are more akin to apprentices than lone scientists. They are apprenticed to more experienced people who guide them and share with them knowledge and skills of their culture (Doherty and Hughes, 2009). It is the joint activity between the two of them that enables children to re-create the culture around them. Social constructivists, especially those in Western culture, argue that children are, and must be seen as active constructors of their own lives. Their voices are important and should be heard, and this has been more and more recognised by doctors, social workers and teachers (Smith et al., 2003). Children's views should be taken into account in all aspects of their lives.

Piagetian theory suggests that children's development is separate from learning. The belief is that learning trails behind development as children cannot understand new concepts until the relevant developmental stage is reached. In contrast, Vygotsky understood learning and development to be mutually dependent and interactive. He proposed the now well-known concept of the 'zone of proximal development' (ZPD) to illustrate what he considered the connection between development and learning. He argued that there is a perceptible gap between what children can achieve independently and what they can achieve with support from a more experienced person. This gap is the zone where learning can take place. Learning that is too easy will not stretch children, and learning that is too hard will not be understandable and so the best place for the learning to take place is in that zone, especially when it builds just sufficiently on prior understanding. The width of the zone indicates how fast and how much children can learn from their 'teachers' (Vygotsky, 1987). Children's learning needs to be organised and structured by teachers to provide an environment (inside the zone of proximal development) within which children can derive the most benefit (Bancroft and Carr, 1995).

A brief consideration of theories of language acquisition can contribute to understanding interactive approaches to teaching and learning. A behaviourist perspective on language development emphasises the importance of children imitating the language of people around them. According to the theory, adults reinforce the sounds children make and gradually these sounds become more and more recognisable as the words, phrases and sentences that make up adult language. Other perspectives assume that learning every word and grammatical construction through imitation and shaping would take much too long and does not account for the speed at which language is learned. Nativists such as Chomsky (1980) suggest that children are biologically predisposed to learning language and have a language acquisition device (LAD) which acts as a mechanism to enable new words and sentences to be used when they have never been heard. Interactionism provides a third view within which is recognised the importance of parents and other adults providing social support and contexts for developing language. Bruner (1983) introduced a 'language acquisition support system' (LASS) through which adults can 'scaffold' children's language learning. They can provide an environment which encourages children to use language; demonstrate more advanced vocabulary and grammatical structure, and expand or re-cast what children say to take them on to the next step. For example, a child says 'cat runned' and the mother expands and re-casts that phrase into 'Yes, the cat did run away, didn't she?' The mother is not correcting the child directly, nor does she demand an imitation of the correct sentence. She is encouraging the language that is being used, demonstrating more advanced structure and keeping the conversation going.

It seems likely that the three perspectives briefly described in the previous paragraph need to be combined to provide a satisfactory explanation of language development. Brain scans have suggested that there are particular areas of the brain that are activated when learning or using language but that, if damaged, other areas of the brain can take over. Brain plasticity can enable new connections to be made between neurons. There is also some evidence to suggest that there is a critical period for language learning, which if missed is likely to limit later language development. Such evidence does seem to point to a biological predisposition to language learning but it cannot account for everything about language learning. Children need an environment that can encourage that innate ability: an environment that is interactive, where people around them talk to them, listen to them and generally encourage all attempts at communication (Doherty and Hughes, 2009).

The Bristol study of young children developing language provides an excellent example of the importance of an interactive approach to teaching and learning. Wells (1986) made a large number of tape recordings of children talking with their mothers and later with teachers in nursery school, and from these natural recordings he suggested that the children who developed the richest language were those who had plenty of opportunities to have conversations with more experienced talkers. One of the most important aspects of these conversations were that adults *listened* to the children. Where adults were didactic in their language teaching or ignored what their children were saying, children's language was less well developed. When they listened to what their children were saying and responded, perhaps by gently expanding on that, then the children's language was more advanced. Wells's results suggest that, on its own, social class does not dictate the richness of language developed by young children. Working-class parents are just as able to listen to their children talking and provide scaffolding to learn new language as middle-class parents – and both working-class and middle-class parents can provide sterile conditions with few interactions and, crucially, few responses to their children's attempts to talk.

Although competence in language is not necessarily connected with social class, many children come to school in the twenty-first century with what are considered to be great disadvantage. Weizman and Snow (2001) investigated the home language of children aged 5, finding that families who share the culture that promotes the importance of education provide the language most likely to be heard and used in schools. According to an I CAN survey in 2004, 89 per cent of nursery staff are worried about children's speaking and listening skills, feeling that the occurrence of speech, language and communication difficulties among pre-school children is growing. Ninety-two per cent felt that the key reason for this situation was the lack of adult and child time spent talking together. The current I CAN website (April 2010) suggests that 40–50 per cent of children start primary school without the basic speech and language skills they need to learn and make friends. The Talk to Your Baby campaign encourages parents to talk to their children from birth so that they can become good communicators, do well at school and lead happy, fulfilled and successful lives (www.literacytrust.org.uk/talk_to_your_baby).

From this selective brief examination of child development, it is clear that interaction is vitally important not just to making sense of that development but also to facilitating the development to occur in the best possible way. Children cannot develop entirely on their own: it is not just biologically driven. They need others to help them to reach maturity in terms of socialisation, emotional development, language and cognition. Others help children to learn and in the next section, there will be examination of interactive approaches in relation to teaching and learning. This first section, deliberately confined discussions to very young infants as early development has been shown to be helpful when understanding the needs of older people with profound disabilities. In the next section pedagogy is examined generally in terms of interactive approaches, but the greatest emphasis is put on early years practice, starting with the importance of using play as a pedagogic tool.

Interactive approaches to pedagogy

It was established at the beginning of this chapter that interactive approaches to teaching and learning promote the importance of children being seen as active learners. They need to be actively engaging with the world and striving to understand the evidence of their senses. They need also to be in control of their own learning and forcing children to learn something in which they have no interest is counterproductive. Probably the most interactive learning is seen in good early years provision for play. Hurst and Joseph's (1998) book has this for a preface: 'active exploration leads to learning' accompanied by a photograph of a toddler playing with a wooden track and vehicles on the floor. The toddler is concentrating on trying to place a length of track in front of him. He seems to be totally absorbed in learning about the properties of objects and what he can make them do. Later in the preface, Hurst and Joseph list the principles for a developmental curriculum which includes 'the role of the educator of young children is to engage actively with what most concerns the child, and to support learning through these preoccupations' (Hurst and Joseph, 1998: xi). It is abundantly clear that active learning is considered fundamental to early learning.

Play is described as being 'freely chosen by the child, and under the control of the child. The child decides how to play, how long to sustain the play, what the play is about, and who to play with' (DCSF, 2009: 10). In this DCSF (2009) document, play is promoted as helping children to develop positive dispositions for learning, such as being engaged and involved, being willing to explore, experiment and try things out and being inventive – creating problems and finding solutions. Adults are encouraged to join in the play sensitively and appropriately so that they can enhance the play and thus the learning. Enhancement involves working within the child's zone of proximal development. It requires teachers to locate individual children's current understanding and through scaffolding, such as questioning and suggestions, help the child to progress to new understanding. It is a tough role for teachers to perform without taking over and showing children how to play or organising the activity so that it ceases to be opportunities for children to engage in their *own* play (Forbes, 2004). Bruce (1991) describes 'free-flow play' which gives children the freedom to follow their own ideas and interests in their own way and for their own reasons. There is no identified end product or criteria to meet and it occurs when children are able to use their experience of ideas, feelings, relationships and movement, and are able to apply them with control, competence and mastery. Emotions play an important part and children are helped to deal with grief, loss and anger through their free-flow play.

One of the playthings developed by Goldschmied (1989) is the 'treasure basket' from which a young child can learn about the cultural objects which can be contained within it. Objects placed in the basket should be available in the child's environment and of a size that they are safe for babies to pick up, wave about, mouth, bang, pull at and drop again, but of course, not small enough to be swallowed. Natural objects such as a shell, a pine cone, a dried gourd and a cork block can accompany kitchen implements, paint brushes, curtain rings and other household items. According to Goldschmied (1989) the adult's role is to sit close to the baby at the treasure basket and provide reassurance and support. From this vantage point, adults can note the emergence of new schema as objects are chosen to be explored. Babies observed while exploring objects show how they are able to interact with those around them by glancing and gazing intently, through little noises, exchanging objects and mutual touching. The close relationship between babies and other people is vital for developing communication and cognition, and sensitive adults can provide the support required, being careful to take the lead from the child, rather than being didactic (Forbes, 2004).

Working with young children with profound disabilities in schools and nurseries can offer a stark contrast to the child-led play described above. First, many young children with profound disabilities have physical disabilities. They may also have visual and/or hearing impairments which make exploring the environment very difficult. Sitting at a treasure basket may be impossible without a huge amount of support and, even then, children may be unable to reach for objects, hold them or, if their muscle tone is very high, they may be unable to drop objects. They may not be able to see the objects or hear the noises they make as they explore them. In these circumstances it is very hard for children to be active in their learning or show which schema are developing. Adults, instead of following the child may need to take a much more leading role. They may need to select objects and maybe even hold the child's hands around those objects or rub the object across the child's skin, shake objects to make them rattle or hold them up for the child to see. In those circumstances, the amount of information available to the child is very limited, making learning from exploration extremely difficult.

Enabling children to move to explore, to use residual vision and hearing, and generally trying to control their own environment, is as vital for children with profound disabilities, however disabled they are. Although correct positioning is important to prevent contractures leading to a twisted body shape, it is important for adults to help children to move independently if possible as they will then be able to play with the freedom suggested at the beginning of this section. If independent movement is not possible then the philosophy of MOVE practitioners (www.move-europe.org.uk/) is to use whatever equipment is necessary to enable movement. According to the website, Oliver spent all day lying on the floor or strapped in a chair until he started the MOVE programme. Now he uses a gait-trainer (a walking frame) to walk around for most of the day. He can stand at tables for various activities and can join in games in the playground. He has the freedom to go where and when he wants. With this movement has come a greater interest in objects in the environment and Oliver can now transfer objects from hand to hand across his midline, holding them up for visual inspection.

Alongside the possible physical and sensory impairments experienced by young children with profound disabilities, by definition these children have enormous difficulties with cognition. They are likely to have a very slow speed of information processing, poor attention skills, a very small working memory and particular difficulties with generalising what they do learn in one situation to another (Dockrell and McShane, 1992). Progress is likely to be extremely slow and there is need for a huge amount of repetition for learning to take place. Adult scaffolding needs to be very precise as the ZPD for children with profound disabilities is likely to be very small. Locating the exact ZPD can be very difficult but can be aided by the Routes for Learning assessment tool (Welsh Assembly Government, 2006). This assessment is composed of communication and cognition development in the first year of life divided into 43 different behaviours that can be observed. The tool also provides some strategies for moving children on to each of the behaviours. The adult can get a reasonably accurate picture of the child's current understanding, although the profound disabilities experienced by the child can mask detail. Another difficulty is that children can show, for example, object permanence with one object but not with any others. For example, Kyle can find chocolate buttons under bowls and pieces of material but he has not looked for any other object. So does he understand object permanence or not? And should the teaching move on with chocolate buttons or stay at this level with other objects? Both are likely to be important.

So far, active learning has been explored entirely from an early years perspective as this seems to be the most relevant for learners with profound disabilities, whatever their chronological age. Many teachers and supporters of older learners with profound disabilities have no difficulties with continuing to support exploration of the world and informal communication beyond the early years, but others are anxious to respond to the pressure to provide 'age appropriate' activities. Instead of continuing to follow the learners' needs, they use complex language, discourage touch and colourful objects and expect complicated activities such as shopping to be understood because that is an adult activity. Active learning through exploration associated with young babies can go on being relevant whatever the actual age of the person.

Despite the seeming irrelevance of 'age appropriateness' to people with profound disabilities, being supported to partake in activities that are potentially far too complicated to be understood can provide rich opportunities to learn interactively. The story and drama work of Grove (2006) and Park (2004) demonstrate how people can be supported to participate in interactive games based on, for example, Greek myths, Shakespeare plays and Dickens novels. Understanding the plots and characters is not the aim of the activities. Aims do include engagement in and enjoying being with other people while experiencing the rhythm of language and short repetitive episodes. It is clear from the reactions of people with profound disabilities that full understanding is far less important than being part of an interactive game where your presence is valued. For example, Katie 'told' an audience about her enjoyment of going out for the day with her family. Katie has profound and multiple learning disabilities but it was clear that she was telling the story herself, through her mother. Her mother had a bag of objects that were very familiar to Katie and represented the different aspects of her days out. Her mother produced each object, to the delight of Katie, and told the audience why it was important to the day out. Katie moved her arms and legs excitedly, made little noises and smiled broadly as, co-actively, they told the story. This was an excellent example of an interactive approach in action.

Working co-actively has long been a method of working with deaf-blind children (who may or may not have profound learning disabilities). Sitting behind the deaf-blind child to enable the close contact required for learning from another person can be very effective. Not only can the children feel the physical process but they can also experience how together with the adult, they can have effect on the world. This is described as the 'van Dijk approach' which emphasises movement-based learning through the stages of resonance, co-active movement, modelling and imitation (Murdoch, 2009). Nafstad and Rodbroe (1999) apply the co-active approach to learning to communicate. They describe a project where they show how communication can be co-constructed between the learner and partner. They describe the process thus:

1   The child presents a movement or sound that the adult perceives like an utterance.

2   The adult confirms that he perceives the movement or sound like an utterance (often by way of imitation).

3   The adult suggests an interpretation to the child (usually imitation plus expansion).

4   The adult gives the child a turn: waits for the child to accept or reject this interpretation.

5   The child accepts or rejects the suggested interpretation (shown by bodily behaviour; smiles or persists, protests, frowns, freezes).

The negotiations that proceed in this way build a repertoire of spontaneous expressions that can be transformed into potentially meaningful utterances in a shared vocabulary. The negotiation is organised as small conversations which are basic to the co-construction of meaning. Nelson (1986) calls these kinds of conversations 'scripts', which are the routines that are repeated many times, for example, peekaboo, little rhymes and stories or a daily episode such as putting on a coat and getting into the pushchair and going shopping. The sheer repetition of these scripts can be very supportive in establishing the pattern of 'You do this: I do this: we do this together'.

Teaching learners with profound disabilities (maybe with multiple impairments) is both specialised and universal. The universality is mainly about 'good teaching', teaching that makes a difference to the lives of learners. Alexander (2010) suggests that, from evidence presented to the Cambridge Primary Review, good teaching:

- is well organised and planned
- is reflective
- is based on sound subject knowledge
- depends on effective classroom management
- requires an understanding of children's developmental needs
- uses exciting and varied approaches
- inspires
- encourages children to become autonomous learners
- facilitates children's learning
- stimulates children's creativity and imagination.

He also suggests that good teaching cannot be tied to prescription, such as that found in the Primary Strategies in recent years (http://nationalstrategies.standards.dcsf.gov.uk/primary/). What good teachers require is the encouragement and support to be creative in meeting needs. The report goes on to extol the importance of many of the components of interactive approaches to pedagogy, such as listening to children's voices, building on children's interests and children taking the lead in their own learning.

Good teaching in classrooms for learners with profound disability enables teachers to value 'talk' which is seen as a mode through which learning takes place. Talk at this level relates to body language, little noises and gestures, and questions are conveyed by voice tone, pointing and joint attention. Questions that learners with profound disabilities can 'answer' are likely to be extremely basic and part of 'your turn: my turn' scripts. An essential tool used by teachers at the earliest level is a 'burst-pause' sequence where the adult provides a burst of activity (a turn) followed by a period of waiting (the other person's turn). The pace of the burst-pause will depend entirely on the pace of the learner's reactions. At this early stage often the turns will be teacher initiated, providing a game such as 'Row the Boat' and after establishing the script will stop to 'ask a question' and wait for an answer. The sequence is a prototype dialogue and it is just as essential in good teaching for learners with profound disabilities as higher order questioning is for typical learners.

☐ Summary

There has been space for only a few examples of interactive approaches to pedagogy but, hopefully, they have demonstrated how the principles of active learning and learners taking control within the development of communication and cognition can be as important to learners with profound disabilities as to typical learners. Motivation has not directly been mentioned but it is clear that people learn best when they are motivated. Kyle is motivated by chocolate, Katie by her favourite objects and Oliver by his new-found ability to move around. They are having fun and are thus engaged happily in the learning process. Sometimes, with people with profound disabilities it is hard to find things that motivate. It is important to keep trying so that when found, these motivating activities can be used centrally in the learning process.

Interactive approaches to teaching and learning became important to educating children with profound learning disabilities in the 1980s. Prior to that time, the dominant theory of learning was behaviourist in nature. Skills to be learned were set by teachers following an analysis of the tasks to be completed and practised until all the steps were mastered. There was no attempt to start teaching from the interest of the child, although task analysis did enable teachers to assess which of the learning steps children needed to master to complete the task. Working in this manner seemed very mechanical and often resulted in children learning skills that they did not always understand, especially when it was applied to learning about communication.

The interactive approaches movement encouraged teachers to seek for pedagogy where understanding the world was at the centre. Intensive interaction is a specific example of how this has been developed with learners who have profound learning disabilities. The rest of this book focuses on the detail of Intensive Interaction, showing how the principles of interactive approaches underpin practice. Intensive interaction has been, without doubt, the most successful method of communicating with both children and adults with profound disabilities and hopefully exploring underlying principles has been helpful.

References

Alexander, R. (ed.) (2010) *Children, Their World, Their Education: Final Report and Recommendations of the Cambridge Primary Review.* London: Routledge.

Bancroft, D. and Carr, R. (1995) *Influencing Children's Development.* Milton Keynes: Open University Press.

Bruce, T. (1991) *Time to Play in Early Childhood Education.* London: Hodder and Stoughton.

Bruner, J. (1983) *Child's Talk: Learning to Use Language.* New York: Norton.

Chomsky, N. (1980) *Language and Learning: The Debate between Jean Piaget and Noam Chomsky.* Cambridge: Harvard University Press.

Collis, M. and Lacey, P. (1996) *Interactive Approaches to Teaching: A Framework for INSET.* London: David Fulton.

De Witt, M. (2009) *The Young Child in Context: A Thematic Approach.* Pretoria: Van Schaik.

Department for Children, Schools and Families (DCSF) (2009) *Learning, Playing and Interacting: Good Practice in the Early Years Foundation Stage.* London: DCSF.

Dockrell, J. and McShane, J. (1992) *Children's Learning Difficulties.* Oxford: Blackwell.

Doherty, J. and Hughes, M. (2009) *Child Development: Theory and Practice 0–11.* Harlow: Pearson Education.

Forbes, R. (2004) *Beginning to Play.* Maidenhead: Open University Press.

Foxen, T. and McBrien, J. (1981) *The EDY In-service Course for Mental Handicap Practitioners: Staff Training in Behavioural Methods.* Manchester: Manchester University Press.

Glenn, S. (1987) 'Interactive approaches to working with children with PMLD', in B. Smith (ed.), *Interactive Approaches to the Education of Children with Severe Learning Difficulties.* Birmingham: Westhill College.

Goldschmied, E. (1989) 'Play and learning in the first year of life', in V. Williams (ed.), *Babies in Day Care: An Examination of the Issues.* London: The Daycare Trust.

Goswami, U. (2008) *Cognitive Development: The Learning Brain.* Hove: Psychology Press.

Grove, N. (2006) *Ways into Literature.* London: David Fulton.

Harris, J. (1987) 'Interactive styles for language facilitation', in B. Smith (ed.), *Interactive Approaches to the Education of Children with Severe Learning Difficulties.* Birmingham: Westhill College.

Hewett, D. and Nind, M. (1987) 'Developing an interactive curriculum for pupils with severe and complex learning difficulties: a classroom process', in B. Smith (ed.), *Interactive Approaches to the Education of Children with Severe Learning Difficulties.* Birmingham: Westhill College.

Hurst, V. and Joseph, J. (1998) *Supporting Early Learning: The Way Forward.* Milton Keynes: Open University Press.

I CAN (2004) Nursery workers' poll says 'Turn off the TV': www.literacytrust. org.uk/talk_to_your_baby/about (accessed April 2010).

Lacey, P. (1987) 'Project work with children with severe learning difficulties', in B. Smith (ed.), *Interactive Approaches to the Education of Children with Severe Learning Difficulties.* Birmingham: Westhill College.

McConkey, R. (1981) 'Education without understanding?', *Special Education,* 8(3): 8–10.

Murdoch, H. (2009) *A Curriculum for Multi-sensory Impaired Children.* London: Sense.

Nafstad, A. and Rodbroe, I. (1999) *Co-Creating Communication: Perspectives on Diagnostic Education for Individuals Who Are Congenitally Deafblind and Individuals Whose Impairments May Have Similar Effect.* Dronninglund: Forlaget Nord-Press.

Nelson, K. (1986) *Event Knowledge: Structure and Function in Development.* Hillside, NJ: Laurence Erlbaum Associates.

Park, K. (2004) *Interactive Storytelling.* Bicester: Speechmark.

Seligman, M. (1975) *Helplessness: On Depression, Development and Death.* San Francisco, CA: Freeman.

Smith, B. (ed.) (1987) *Interactive Approaches to the Education of Children with Severe Learning Difficulties.* Birmingham: Westhill College.

Smith, B. (ed.) (1990) *Interactive Approaches to Teaching the Core Subjects: The National Curriculum for Pupils with Severe and Moderate Learning Difficulties.* Birmingham: Westhill College.

Smith, B., Moore, Y. and Phillips, C. (1983) 'Education with understanding', *Special Education*, 10(2): 21–4.

Smith, P., Cowie, H. and Blades, M. (2003) *Understanding Children's Development.* Oxford: Blackwell.

Vygotsky, L. (1987) *Thinking and Speech.* New York: Plenum.

Weizman, Z. and Snow, C. (2001) 'Lexical output as it relates to children's vocabulary acquisition: effects of sophisticated exposure as a support for meaning', *Developmental Psychology*, 37: 265–79.

Wells, G. (1986) *The Meaning Makers.* London: Hodder and Stoughton.

Welsh Assembly Government (2006) *Routes for Learning: Assessment Material for Learners with Profound Learning Difficulties and Additional Disabilities.* Cardiff: Welsh Assembly Government.

4

Wired for communication: how the neuroscience of infancy helps in understanding the effectiveness of Intensive Interaction

M. Suzanne Zeedyk

Chapter overview

The aim of this chapter is to describe some of the insights that have been gained in regard to infant behaviour and brain development. This will highlight just how fundamental the capacity for communication is and how attuned we are, as people, to a sense of emotional connection with others. What Intensive Interaction allows us to see is that this capacity is retained even when individuals have difficulty demonstrating it, as a consequence of communicative impairments such as autism, learning disabilities or dementia. Indeed, to my mind, the power of Intensive Interaction is not only that it provides a practical means of reaching people with communicative difficulties, but that it yields a fundamental rethink of what we mean by 'communicative disorders'. It prompts us to realise that a communicative problem lies not within an individual person, but in the space between two people. From this fresh perspective, new vistas open up, and it becomes easy to see how it is that frustrating interactions can be turned into joyful ones. I end the chapter by exploring such conceptual issues, for they illuminate the kinds of questions that the field of Intensive Interaction is now well placed to ask of itself and related fields.

The psychological and neurological sciences have, over the past several decades, revealed two key insights about human development. These are that infants come into the world already connected to other people, and that the pathways in their brains are literally moulded by the responses they receive from those around them. The bulk of the excitement following from these findings has focused on the early years: what children need between the ages of birth and 3 years in order to give them the best long-term life chances. I think, though, that these findings also go a long way towards explaining why Intensive Interaction, and other interactive approaches like it, are effective in nurturing the communicative abilities of individuals struggling to engage with others. They help us to appreciate that Intensive Interaction is tapping into processes that lie at the core of our humanity.

Infants' innate capacity for connection

Infants have an innate capacity for connection. They are born already exhibiting an awareness of and sensitivity to other people's attention and movements. They arrive tuned into the sounds and voices that became familiar while they were in the womb. They engage in turn-taking exchanges, and they become distressed if their partner fails to take their turn in that exchange. They coordinate the rhythm of their movements with the rhythm of their partner's speech. In short, infants do not need to learn how to engage with other people. This is a capacity they possess innately. Evolutionary forces have ensured that, at our core, humans are social beings, and neuroscience is helping us to realise how the very construction of our brains is influenced by the way other people respond to us.

What types of studies have been carried out to uncover infants' social sensitivities? One area of research that has proven particularly significant is that of imitation. Within minutes of birth, infants are able to imitate facial expressions such as tongue protrusion, mouth opening, and lip pursing. This was first demonstrated in the 1970s (Maratos, 1973; Meltzoff and Moore, 1977), and has since generated a wealth of experimental studies and animated debate. We know that neonates imitate sounds and gestures (for example, Kokkinaki and Kugiumutzakis, 2000; Meltzoff and Moore, 1989). They can carry out a series of different imitative acts, for example following their partner's lead by extending first one finger, then two fingers, then three fingers (Nagy et al., 2005). Their very physiology is oriented to such exchanges (Nagy and Molnar, 2004), in that their heart rate decreases when they take their turn (for example, copying a one-finger extension), and increases while they wait to see what their partner will do when they take their turn (for example, continue with another one-finger extension?; change to a new topic like a two-finger extension?; not respond at all?). Theorists have argued about whether this imitative ability is a cognitive process, a perceptual process, or perhaps a reflex (for overviews, see Hurley and Chater, 2005; Meltzoff and Prinz, 2002). My own interpretation is that imitation is an emotional process, a view shared by Kugiumutzakis (1998), Trevarthen (2008) and Nagy (2006), among others. When you are imitated by someone else, you experience yourself as heard, as known. There is an intimacy associated with two people acknowledging, through the mirroring of their actions, that they are jointly focused on one another (Zeedyk, 2006). Imitative exchanges are not acts of copying, but moments of sharing.

Another area of research that has helped in revealing the innate connectedness of babies is the still face paradigm. In this procedure, parents (usually mothers) engage in a typical exchange with their baby, followed by a period of several minutes where they refrain from responding, by holding their face still (Adamson and Frick, 2003). Findings show that infants detect this change, and that they find it uncomfortable. They quickly go from a joyous expression to a more sober one, followed by an attempt to re-engage their mother through smiling at her, but when their mother fails to respond, they disengage, look away, get fretful and may cry. This process of change is rapid, taking place over less than a minute, and mothers often report that they, too, find it uncomfortable and difficult. They do not like ignoring their baby's request for interaction. While this procedure was first developed for use with older infants (3 months or older), Nagy (2008) has recently been using it with neonates. She has shown that newborns, only a few days old, exhibit the same pattern of attempting to engage and then withdrawing. This demonstrates that the rhythm and 'signals' of social engagement are not something that babies learn about over time; it is an innate sensitivity with which they are born.

Infants bring with them early social preferences, too. Classic studies carried out in the 1980s showed that infants become familiar with the sounds of their world while still in the womb, and that those sounds can later be used to comfort them. For example, DeCasper and Spence (1986) had pregnant women read a story to their 'bump' every day for the last six weeks of their pregnancy. It was always the same story: *The Cat in the Hat*, by Dr Seuss. Within the first few days after birth, the research team played a recording of the mother reading either that same story or a different story, while the infants sucked an electronically monitored nipple. Findings showed that infants sucked more rapidly in response to the story their mother had been reading, thus indicating that they were already familiar with it. The infants even could distinguish between recordings of their own mother and another woman reading the same story, as well as detect when their mother replaced the phrase 'cat in the hat' with 'dog in the fog'. This is how sensitive babies' awareness is; at less than 3 days old, they can distinguish between subtle vowel sounds, even when the rhythm of the story stays the same.

This has been only a brief review of the types of studies that have been carried out in the psychological literature on neonates. There are numerous others, such as those showing that infants are born already familiar with their mothers' smell (Varendi et al., 1994), that being touched facilitates infants' growth (Field, 2001), and that at only a few days old, infants can already discriminate their mother's face from a stranger's (Pascalis et al., 1995). In short, babies have a wide array of abilities available to them at birth that enable them to participate actively in social interactions. They do not have to wait to learn these abilities, via cognitive maturation or because parents mistakenly 'impute intentionality' to their babies' actions (for example, Schaffer, 1977; see Zeedyk, 1996, for discussion). Infants arrive already emotionally connected to other people. Indeed, the foetal literature suggests that they are already connected to *particular* other people – the people whose voices, rhythms, and smells have become familiar to them in the womb. As Colwyn Trevarthen (2008: 35), one of the seminal theorists in this field, summarises it: 'All human beings, even the youngest, oldest, and the most impaired in capacities of communication, retain motives to find and share meaning.'

Brain development

If developmental psychology has been busy revealing the sophistication of infant capacities, then neuroscience has been revealing how those capacities contribute to infants' brain development. Two of the important points emerging from neuroscientific research over the past several decades are that brain growth occurs more rapidly between conception and 3 years than it ever will again and that brain growth is shaped by the experiences that infants have of the world around them, especially social experiences. The clinical psychologist Sue Gerhardt (2005) puts it this way: 'The human baby is incomplete. It arrives ready to be programmed by adults.'

Humans are born with immature brains. While organs like hearts and lungs are largely fully formed at birth, brains are not. This allows infant brains to develop in relation to whatever environment they find themselves, so that they become well suited to that particular environment. A brain can thus adapt to a world that speaks any language (for example, English or Japanese or Urdu), to a world that is predictable or one that is unpredictable (for example, a family where comfort is reliably available versus one where there is domestic violence), or to a world where touch is frequent versus less constant (for example, a culture where strollers are frequently used versus one where infants are carried next to a parent's body). Adaptability is an advantage of immature brains, although this leaves infant brains extremely vulnerable to stressful, threatening environments. Other mammals are born with brains that are more mature, and thus less adaptable but also less vulnerable.

Human brains continue to develop and shape and reshape themselves throughout childhood and adolescence (and even to some extent in adulthood). It is easy to think of this as occurring in three main stages. The first is from conception to about age 3. This is the period of most rapid development, when neural pathways are exploding. Brains develop not through acquiring new cells (that is, neurons), but through forming connections between cells (that is, synapses). With every experience an infant has, the brain creates synapses. Each time an experience reoccurs, that synaptic connection is strengthened. That is the implication of the quip 'neurons that fire together, wire together'.

So, when an infant feels distressed and cries, if they are regularly picked up by someone familiar, then a pathway to calmness is formed in their brain. Alternatively, if they are regularly left to cry on their own, then a pathway to anxiety is formed. Since infants come into the world already aware of connection with other people, it follows that to receive a response from others is calming; conversely, to regularly experience non-responsiveness provokes anxiety. A child can cope with anxiety, but operating in this way is more effortful than it would be under other conditions. It is analogous to having a back injury. If we are experiencing back pain, we will survive, but life will be more wearing and less enjoyable than if we were not having to cope with that distress. Brains that become wired for anxiety and emotional disconnection produce a more wearing, less rich experience of life than do brains that become wired for calmness and connection.

The next major stage of brain development occurs between roughly 5 and 12 years. By the time this stage begins, children have formed robust pathways in their brain. They have worked out how their world functions. They know whether it is a safe, reliable one, in which they can take for granted that their emotional – and thus physiological – needs will be met, or whether they live in an unpredictable, anxious world, where they have to spend energy being on their guard. Their brain will have developed a set of neural pathways that helps them to cope with either extreme. It has learned which messages are most frequently sent. The explosion of synapses can slow down. Neurological development now shifts to strengthening further the existing connections, a process known as myelination. This allows messages to be transmitted even more efficiently. If neural pathways to calmness have been laid down, then those are the pathways the brain will tend to use in making sense of the world. Similarly, if robust pathways to anxiety have been established, then those are the pathways the brain will resort to most quickly. In short, this second stage of brain development is focused on increasing neural efficiency.

The final stage occurs during adolescence. The brain has one last burst of synapse creation in this period, while sharply increasing its rate of pruning. Synapses that are left over from earlier stages, but that are never used, are sloughed off. Getting rid of these neural dead ends heightens efficiency even further. The adult brain is able to process the messages it receives (that is, the experiences that the person has) as rapidly and automatically as possible. It will, of course, be using the pathways that have become most robust during earlier stages – such as those pathways to calmness or anxiety.

The three-stage description I have given for brain development is intentionally simplified. Processes such as synaptic formation, proliferation and pruning are actually ongoing. It would be more accurate to say that the proportion of these processes alters over time, with the rate of synapse pruning increasingly outstripping the rate of synapse formation as a person gets older. (Indeed, as we grow from adolescence into adulthood and then into old age, that ratio of pruning to formation gets painfully steep!) It would also be possible to tell the story of brain development with a number of sub-stages. For example, pathways in the visual cortex develop almost entirely during the first year; pathways for language development are largely in place by 5 years of age. Such periods thus offer windows of opportunity or 'hot spots' for influencing most fully the development of associated skills and abilities. (For extended descriptions of brain development, see Gerhardt, 2005; Kotaluk, 1996.)

It is worth commenting on two final insights that neuroscience has yielded. The first is that it is not only synaptic pathways that are being established in the early years. Baselines for the production of hormones and neurotransmitters are also being established. This includes the stress hormone cortisol, the relaxation hormone oxytocin, the happiness hormone serotonin and the reward-seeking hormone dopamine. So, for example, if a child lives in a stressful environment, her body learns to rapidly produce cortisol, which is useful in helping the body to cope with acute stress, but which is damaging if chronically produced. If a child lives in an environment where lots of cuddling is available (but not forced), then his body learns to rapidly produce the hormone oxytocin, which generates a sense of calm and increases the capacity for empathy with others. Thus, the hormone baselines that are established during the early years are likely to be the same ones in use during later years, unless adults take active steps to alter those baselines, through techniques such as meditation, yoga or exercise.

A second insight is that play is critical to neural generation. It needs to be free play: active, unstructured, dynamic, relaxed. The saying that 'a child's job is play' captures the importance of being able to explore the world at a pace and with a focus that suits one's own rhythm. Dynamic systems theory (Thelen, 2000) has pointed this out for some years, arguing that the systems of the body and mind work in conjunction. Thus, the rhythms of a child's movements are linked to her feeding routines, the speech she hears, the pace of her vocal exchanges with her parents and the postural adjustments she makes while being transported. Of course, these all go on to influence her cognitive and emotional capacities. The central point of dynamic systems theory is that interactions among parts of a system induce organisational changes in the whole. Neuroscience has built on this platform, and is now revealing that free play is critical for the very generation of neural synapses (Kotaluk, 1996). While all experiences will foster neural connection, free play seems to be particularly important because it is creative. Creativity sparks a much larger number of synapses than does directed play. When children are free to re-experience what interests them, those synaptic connections are strengthened. It is ironic that, as society comes to understand more about the importance of play, children have fewer and fewer options to engage in such creative activity. And in the context of this chapter, it is ironic that so many interventions for people with learning difficulties have been prescriptive and essentially non-creative.

Intensive Interaction

The findings I have been exploring enrich our understanding of why Intensive Interaction works. This approach tells us about much more than simply the treatment of learning disabilities. It drives home the insight that emotional connection is central to our sense of our own humanity.

This focus on the nature of humanity leads to a more expansive vision of Intensive Interaction than is typical. Intensive Interaction began as a novel means of working with individuals institutionalised due to some sort of learning disability or special needs (for example, Caldwell, 2006; Ephraim, 1979; Nind and Hewett, 2005). It was more creative, flexible and playful than the directive approaches that dominated in the 1970s and 1980s. Since then, its effectiveness has resulted in a geographical and conceptual explosion. Intensive Interaction is now enthusiastically practised throughout the UK and beyond (including Australia, New Zealand, Eastern Europe, Czech Republic, Montenegro and Thailand). It has successfully challenged the understanding of labels such as 'severe learning difficulties' and 'severe autism', preventing anyone from automatically assuming that they mean the person concerned has no capacity for communication. Intensive Interaction has indeed, as Jeffries (2009: 58) asserts, 'come of age ... and its potential benefits are thrilling to many who use the approach'.

And yet, its reach may have only begun. The insights that are being generated within the Intensive Interaction community take us well beyond the disabilities field. They place us in a philosophical realm, urging us to think more deeply about what it means to call ourselves a social species. They point to important gaps in the current neuroscientific landscape, and they force reflection on the terminology we adopt. In short, Intensive Interaction has the potential to foment fresh understandings of our core humanity.

I make this rather grand claim for three reasons. First, Intensive Interaction is now being shown to be useful for a diverse range of communicative impairments, including not only learning difficulties, autism, and sensory impairment, but also dementia, stroke, brain injury and early social deprivation (for summaries, see Jeffries, 2009; Zeedyk, 2008). It has been suggested as suitable for mothers experiencing postnatal depression, infants born with a cleft palate and even possibly helpful to individuals suffering from phantom limb pain (as an alternative to mirror box therapy (Ramachandran et al., 1995)). How could the same technique be effective for such a wide variety of 'disorders'? One would not immediately expect the treatment of autism, dementia, and postnatal depression to be linked. Yet they are being linked, both theoretically and empirically. This means that Intensive Interaction transcends any specific disorder and taps into deeper qualities, qualities that are central to our experiences as persons relating to other persons. Relational engagement lies at the heart of much philosophical enquiry, particularly as explored by Merleau-Ponty and by Buber.

Second, Intensive Interaction is only one of a number of interactive interventions that have emerged in recent years. Other approaches include co-creative communication (Nafstad and Rodbroe, 1999), floortime (Greenspan et al., 1998), reciprocal imitation training (Ingersoll and Schreibman, 2006), video interactive guidance (Kennedy and Sked, 2008), dance therapy, and music therapy. The core contention of all these approaches is that communication occurs by drawing on joint bodily rhythms, actions and movements, and by turning them into a dialogue. Such choice leads us to ask: how different are these various approaches? Might they actually be presenting the same core message, simply wrapped in different titles? Maybe it does not matter what we call the approach; maybe all that is important is relationship, which is central to all of them. Or maybe the subtle differences between approaches turn out to be important, with some offering more invigorating or effective visions of interaction than do others? Comparative analysis between interactive interventions is rarely undertaken, so we do not yet begin to have answers to such questions. It is important, for the sake of the science as well as the clients, that the field begin to seek some soon.

Finally, the outcomes achieved by Intensive Interaction bear a striking similarity to those reported in several areas of the adult psychological literature. For example, studies on 'non-conscious mimicry' (for example, Chartrand and Bargh, 1999; van Baaren et al., 2004) show that when adults are imitated, though without any conscious awareness that their body movements, postures and breathing rhythms are being copied, then their pro-social attitudes and behaviours increase. They like their partner more, they are more interested in them, they orient their body towards them and they feel happier. These are exactly the kinds of outcomes reported for Intensive Interaction, although there is virtually no cross-referencing between the two literatures and despite the fact that practitioners of Intensive Interaction would certainly decry any use of the term 'mimicry' to describe what they are doing! In the therapeutic field, counsellors are generally taught to 'mirror' their clients and, in marketing, salespeople and call centre staff are taught to 'match' the content and style of their customers' requests. These techniques bear important similarities to Intensive Interaction, but again there is little overlap between the literatures. Intensive Interaction has tended to stay wedded to its original links with the infant literature, without returning to see what contemporary psychology could now tell it. It may be, then, that the impact of engagement is even more comprehensive than the field of Intensive Interaction, or other interactive interventions, have so far estimated.

I see this set of diverse findings as telling us something about what could be termed 'the neuroscience of listening'. It seems that when we experience ourselves as fully heard, fully acknowledged – via a match with the body movements of our partner – then we become more at ease both with ourselves and with that partner (Zeedyk, 2006). The match generates trust, intimacy, spontaneity and a sense of safety. This process is so fundamental that is applies across all age groups and all diagnostic categories, and it is processed subconsciously. Our brains automatically take note of motoric and physiologic similarities with another, and imbue that congruence with emotional significance. Attunement to relationship is embedded in the very fibres of the brain.

My account is supported by the growing knowledge of mirror neurons. Discovered by Rizzolatti's Italian team (Rizzolatti and Craighero, 2004), these are neurons (or, more accurately, neural networks) that fire both when a person has an experience or observes a similar experience occurring in another person. So, the neurons that fire when I move my arm downwards also fire when I see someone else moving their arm downwards. This implies that interpersonal connection is so fundamental to the human species that our brains make use of the same neural networks to process stimuli. You and I are connected at the neural level.

Thus, one way to explain Intensive Interaction's effectiveness is to see it as tapping into mirror neuron systems. The fact that the joyous, calm behaviour we observe as a consequence of Intensive Interaction seems so surprising is a sign that those systems are not being accessed in their daily lives. This means that they do not usually experience themselves as heard. They live lives of emotional isolation. This leads me to wonder, would it really be that hard to institute Intensive Interaction throughout clients' daily lives? Are we talking about something highly specialised, when we talk about Intensive Interaction? No. Are we talking about something difficult or expensive? No. We are simply talking about really excellent listening – something that all of us value. We bloom when we are confident that others are paying attention to us.

Is this, then, a core reason why Intensive Interaction works? Is it that it signals to the brains of clients that they are finally, perhaps for the first time in their life, being listened to? They can relax into this emotional luxury. As anxiety eases, capacities that had been previously obscured can come to the fore, often within minutes – curiosity, attentiveness, humour, language and imitation. Intensive Interaction can begin to be understood not so much as a means of teaching communicative fundamentals, but as creating a context in which existing capacities can flourish. That such sophisticated communicative capacities – anticipation of turn-taking, perception of rhythm and tone, joy in sharing another's presence – should be so rapidly accessible after years of obscurity is a testament to their essential human nature.

My contention is that Intensive Interaction has much more to do with being human than it has to do with impairment. Seeing it in this way allows us to reverse the standard conceptual hierarchy, in which those of us who are not disabled see ourselves as somehow boosting the humanity of those who are. Instead, 'disabled' people reveal something to the rest of us about our sense of our selves.

Conceptual rethink

The line of argument I have presented opens up new lines of thinking for the Intensive Interaction community. I will end this chapter by focusing briefly on two particularly interesting questions that relate to neuroscience: what is the nature of autism and how important is the early diagnosis of developmental delay? Each of these questions turns out to be simultaneously exciting and controversial. That is, of course, the aim of this volume – to extend the boundaries of our current understanding of Intensive Interaction. This innovative approach has been with us for 30 years, and has dramatically altered the way that practitioners can work with and think about communicative disorders. Where do we want to take this movement over the next 30 years?

The nature of autism: does Intensive Interaction point towards a richer understanding?

The cause of autism remains a topic of debate. One of the outcomes of Intensive Interaction is that it points towards a novel explanation, certainly one that is not mainstream. The most popular accounts of autism at present argue that some type of cognitive deficit lies at its core, relating perhaps to theory of mind, executive function or central coherence (for example, Baron-Cohen et al., 1985; Frith, 1989).

Support has been given to these accounts by the suggestion that mirror neuron systems could be 'broken' in autism (Ramachandran and Oberman, 2006). That would explain why people with autism have such difficulty reading other people's feelings and thoughts.

However, if the mirror neuron systems of people with autism are permanently broken, or fundamental deficits exist within their cognitive processes, then we should not gain the outcomes that are repeatedly seen in Intensive Interaction. A large corpus of video material has now been collected within the Intensive Interaction field, depicting people with autism doing all sorts of things they shouldn't be able to do if they have the kind of core cognitive or social deficits described in mainstream accounts of autism. They look at their partner's face, anticipate their response, laugh, tease and take joy in their partner's engagement. Indeed, many of the clients displaying such behaviour had also seemed, at the beginning of the session, to be unable to do them at all. And yet, after only a matter of minutes, they are spontaneously exhibiting a whole range of surprising capacities. Microanalytic analyses of video material have been conducted to confirm such changes, and have revealed quite systematic increases in eye gaze, proximity, orientation and positive emotion (for example, Zeedyk et al., 2009). Such unexpected behavioural shifts point to the need for an alternative explanation of autism.

Phoebe Caldwell (2006, 2010) argues that the answer lies in a sensory account of autism. Practitioners and families repeatedly describe a multitude of hyper- and hypo-sensory problems experienced by people with autism. They cover their ears, bang their heads against the wall, flap their hands in front of their eyes, scream, bite their hand and they can become aggressive if carers try to prevent such behaviours. A sensory account of autism was advanced in the 1970s, and there are a few theorists who continue to argue strongly for it (for example, Bogdashina, 2003), but it is not at present a popular account of autism. Most cognitive theorists conceive sensory problems as secondary, rather than primary, issues in autism.

The outcomes of Intensive Interaction enable us to see how a sensory account could provide a more comprehensive explanation of autism. If Intensive Interaction reduces sensory distress (especially if combined with techniques of sensory integration, as recommended by Caldwell, 2006), then this explains how previously hidden behaviours could spontaneously emerge. These include the social behaviours that are so common with Intensive Interaction, such as gaze to the partner's face, teasing, imitation, joy and calmness, as well as linguistic and cognitive capacities. It can then be argued that people with autism do not have a fundamental deficit in such domains, but that their usual environment is too sensorily distressing to allow these capacities to be demonstrated. When the environment changes, so too does their distress, followed by their behaviour. This explanation can even garner support from some accounts of mirror neurons. Ramachandran and Oberman (2006) suggest that, in autism, mirror neurons may not be broken, but merely obscured by 'autonomic storms'. Autonomic storms are equivalent to the meltdowns described by Caldwell (2006) and innumerable parents and staff members.

Thus, Intensive Interaction has the potential to generate a new understanding of autism. We could see it as a type of anxiety disorder. The environments in which we ask people with autism to live are often painful, confusing and threatening. We need not have intended this; it can result simply from our failure to take seriously their distress. We have classified it as 'challenging behaviour', with the implied need to control and defend against it. If we began to perceive it as 'distressed behaviour', how might our response change? This demonstrates how radical, at its heart, Intensive Interaction can be. From simple linguistic alterations come major conceptual shifts.

Early diagnosis of developmental delay: how important is it?

How important is early diagnosis of developmental disorders such as autism, learning disability and sensory impairment? The answer to this is: incredibly important. Neuroscientific insights about the early proliferation of synaptic connections yield more than a description of brain development. They force us to a realisation that adults are literally shaping the brains of children. We – institutional managers, support staff, policy-makers, product designers and parents – are creating the contexts to which young children's brains must adapt. We are creating the contexts that promote certain types of pathways, as opposed to others. This implies that we may be unintentionally exacerbating autistic tendencies and learning difficulties.

This is an uncomfortable observation. It can feel rather too close to Bettelheim's now-discarded, 1950's explanation that emotionally reserved mothers 'caused' autism. It can imply that poor quality care on the part of support staff or parents is somehow 'causing' learning disabilities. Both these explanations are simplistic – so simplistic that they are wrong.

But I believe there is more to our intense rejection of these explanations than simply their inaccuracy. I think that we are worried about the implications they hold of blame. In today's political climate, we are keen that parents and staff carry no guilt or reproach that they have somehow 'caused' the conditions of the children they love and work with. We are wary of even coming close to such an insinuation. I wonder whether our fear of blame is so great that it is keeping families and practitioners from benefiting as fully as possible from today's neuroscientific discoveries. If we can let go of that fear, then we will be able to think more creatively and insightfully about how to support the development of children with developmental disorders.

We will realise how very important early diagnosis is, because it is in those earliest years, between birth and 3 years – before diagnoses have often been made – that the most rapid, fundamental neural growth is taking place. This is the point at which the intersection of Intensive Interaction and neuroscience becomes especially inviting; it allows us to comprehend the full meaning of 'partnership'. It tells us that we have a chance to change children's life courses for the better, to alter their very biology and brain structure. It tells us that to have a 'disorder' is not to have a preordained biological prison sentence. We now know that brain development is an organic process; it takes place in relation to the world in which the child finds him or herself. What Intensive Interaction allows us to comprehend is how easy it is to begin to change the child's world. We do that through partnership – authentic, attentive relationships.

Intensive Interaction lets us, if we let it, begin to really understand the transformative power of emotional connection.

☐ Summary

My aim in this chapter has been to demonstrate how the insights gained from the study of infant brain development can help us to better understand the effectiveness of Intensive Interaction. As human infants, we come into the world already emotionally connected to other people, and we need to retain that sense of connectedness throughout our lives, in order to have the best chance of maintaining good mental health. Intensive Interaction provides a means of rapidly building relationships with those who have lived long lives of exclusion. The outcomes it yields demonstrate that the need for relationship is as imperative for those with communicative disorders as it is for those without. Thus, Intensive Interaction is more than an approach to intervention. The behavioural changes associated with it prompt a radical rethink of our contemporary explanations of 'disorders' such as autism and dementia. In my view, though, Intensive Interaction takes us even further than this. The shared joy that it generates speaks to the very core of our humanity. It reveals to us, if we let it, the transformative power of emotional connection.

References

Adamson, L.B. and Frick, J.E. (2003) 'The still face: a history of a shared experimental paradigm', *Infancy*, 4: 451–73.

Baron-Cohen, S., Leslie, A.M. and Frith, U. (1985) 'Does the autistic child have a "theory of mind"?', *Cognition*, 21: 37–46.

Bogdashina, O. (2003) *Sensory Perceptual Issues in Autism and Asperger Syndrome*. London: Jessica Kingsley.

Buber, M. (1923/2004) *I and Thou*. London: Continuum.

Caldwell, P. (2006) *Finding You, Finding Me*. London: Jessica Kingsley.

Caldwell, P. (2010) *Autism and Intensive Interaction*. London: Jessica Kingsley.

Chartrand, T.L. and Bargh. J.A. (1999) 'The Chameleon effect: the perception behavior link and social interaction', *Journal of Personality and Social Psychology*, 76: 893–910.

DeCasper, A.J. and Spence, M.J. (1986) 'Prenatal maternal speech influences newborns' perception of speech sounds', *Infant Behavior and Development*, 9: 133–50.

Ephraim, G. (1979) 'Augmented mothering', unpublished paper, Bryn-y-Neuadd Hospital, Llanfairfechan, Gwynedd, North Wales.

Field, T. (2001) *Touch*. Cambridge, MA: MIT Press.

Frith, U. (1989) *Autism: Explaining the Enigma*. Oxford: Blackwell.

Gerhardt, S. (2005) *Why Love Matters: How Affection Shapes a Baby's Brain*. Hove: Routledge.

Greenspan, S.I., Wieder, S. and Simons, R. (1998) *The Child with Special Needs: Encouraging Intellectual and Emotional Growth*. Jackson, TN: Perseus Books.

Hurley, S. and Chater, N. (eds) (2005) *Perspectives on Imitation: From Neuroscience to Social Science*. Cambridge, MA: MIT Press.

Ingersoll, B. and Schreibman, L. (2006) 'Teaching reciprocal imitation skills to young children with autism using a naturalistic behavioural approach', *Journal of Autism and Developmental Disorders*, 36: 487–505.

Jeffries, L. (2009) 'Introducing Intensive Interaction', *The Psychologist*, 22 (September): 788–91.

Kennedy, H. and Sked, H. (2008) 'Video interaction guidance: a bridge to better interactions for individuals with communication impairments', in M.S. Zeedyk (ed.), *Promoting Social Interaction for Individuals with Communicative Impairments: Making Contact*. London: Jessica Kingsley.

Kokkinaki, T. and Kugiumutzakis, G. (2000) 'Basic aspects of vocal imitation in infant–parent interaction during the first six months', *Journal of Reproductive and Infant Psychology*, 18: 173–87.

Kotaluk, R. (1996) *Inside the Brain: Revolutionary Discoveries of How the Brain Works*. Kansas City, KS: Andrews McMeel.

Kugiumutzakis, G. (1998) 'Neonatal imitation in the intersubjective companion space', in S. Bråten (ed.), *Intersubjective Communication and Emotion in Early Ontogeny*. Cambridge: Cambridge University Press.

Maratos, O. (1973) 'The origin and development of imitation in the first six months of life', paper presented at Annual Meeting of the British Psychological Society, Liverpool, ERIC Listing, ED096001.

Meltzoff, A.N. and Moore, M.K. (1977) 'Imitation of facial and manual gestures by human neonates', *Science*, 198: 75–8.

Meltzoff, A.N. and Moore, M.K. (1989) 'Imitation in newborn infants: exploring the range of gestures imitated and the underlying mechanisms', *Developmental Psychology*, 25: 954–62.

Meltzoff, A.N. and Prinz, W. (ed.) (2002) *The Imitative Mind: Development, Evolution, and Brain Bases*. Cambridge: Cambridge University Press.

Merleau-Ponty, M. (1942/1965) *The Structure of Behaviour*. Trans. Alden Fisher. London: Methuen.

Nafstad, A. and Rodbroe, I. (1999) *Co-creating Communication*. Oslo: Forlaget-Nord Press.

Nagy, E. (2006) 'From imitation to conversation: the first dialogues with human neonates', *Infant and Child Development*, 15: 223–32.

Nagy, E. (2008) 'Innate intersubjectivity: newborns' sensitivity to communicative disturbance', *Developmental Psychology*, 44: 1779–84.

Nagy, E. and Molnar, P. (2004) 'Homo imitans or homo provocans? Human imprinting model of neonatal imitation', *Infant Behaviour and Development*, 27: 54–63.

Nagy, E., Compagne, H., Orvos, H., Pal, A., Molnar, P., Janszky, I., Loveland, K.A. and Bardos, G. (2005) 'Index finger movement imitation by human neonates', *Pediatric Research*, 58: 749–53.

Nind, M. and Hewett, D. (2005) *Access to Communication: Developing the Basics of Communication with People with Severe Learning Difficulties through Intensive Interaction*, 2nd edn. London: David Fulton.

Pascalis, O., de Schonen, S., Morten, J., Deruelle, C. and Fabre-Grenet, M. (1995) 'Mother's face recognition by neonates: a replication and an extension', *Infant Behavior and Development*, 18: 79–85.

Ramachandran, V.S., Rogers-Ramachandran, D.C. and Cobb, S. (1995) 'Touching the phantom', *Nature*, 377: 489–90.

Ramachandran, V.S. and Oberman, L.M. (2006) 'Broken mirrors: a theory of autism', *Scientific American*, 295: 39–45.

Rizzolatti, G. and Craighero, L. (2004) 'The mirror-neuron system', *Annual Review of Neuroscience*, 27: 169–92.

Schaffer, R. (1977) *Studies in Mother–Infant Interaction*. London: Academic Press.

Thelen, E. (2000) 'Grounded in the world: developmental origins of the embodied mind', *Infancy*, 1: 3–28.

Trevarthen, C. (2008) 'Intuition for human communication', in M.S. Zeedyk (ed.), *Promoting Social Interaction for Individuals with Communicative Impairments: Making Contact*. London: Jessica Kingsley.

van Baaren, R.B., Holland, R., Kawakami, K. and van Knippenberg, A. (2004) 'Mimicry and pro-social behaviour', *Psychological Science*, 15: 71–4.

Varendi, H., Porter, R. and Winnberg, J. (1994) 'Does the newborn baby find the nipple by smell?', *The Lancet*, 344: 989–90.

Zeedyk, M.S. (1996) 'Developmental accounts of intentionality: toward integration', *Developmental Review*, 16: 416–61.

Zeedyk, M.S. (2006) 'From subjectivity to inter-subjectivity: the transformative roles of emotional intimacy and imitation', *Infant and Child Development*, 15: 321–44.

Zeedyk, M.S. (ed.) (2008) *Promoting Social Interaction for Individuals with Communicative Impairments: Making Contact*. London: Jessica Kingsley.

Zeedyk, M.S., Caldwell, P. and Davies, C.E. (2009) 'How rapidly does Intensive Interaction promote social engagement for adults with profound learning disabilities?', *European Journal of Special Needs Education*, 24: 119–37.

5

Intensive Interaction and its relationship with the triad of impairments in ASD

Lydia Swinton

Chapter overview

The prospect that Intensive Interaction has particular application to people who have autistic spectrum disorder (ASD) will be placed in the context of present theoretical perspectives on the nature of ASD. In particular, the way in which both the learning outcomes and efficacious interactive nature of the teaching and learning sessions addresses the effects of the 'central triad of impairment' will be discussed.

Brief overview of ASD and the definition of the triad

My initial introduction to ASD was during a university course, where the general consensus seemed to be that all people with ASD exhibited the same deficits and strengths – there was no reference to a 'spectrum' of autism, and certainly no mention of the variety of severe and complex needs of many individuals with autism. It was only when I began working with young people with ASD that I realised the range of individual differences and, critically, the vast complexity of trying to teach social skills – those attainments which seem to occur so naturally and effortlessly in neurotypical children. My experience of the approaches used to teach individuals with ASD did not seem to incorporate any means of teaching these social skills or, if they did address the issue of social communication at all, it was in a manner which seemed artificial and formulaic.

I anticipate that all readers will probably be acquainted with the content of this section. However, I will briefly review the conceptualisations of the triad of impairments in autism in order to introduce the central theme: the beneficial partnership between the processes of Intensive Interaction and its outcomes, and our understandings of the social and communication impairments of the triad.

The impairments in social and communication skills in ASD are well documented, dating back to the original work of Kanner (1943, cited in Frith, 2003: 8–9), who used the following deficits as diagnostic features of autism: 'Autistic aloneness' – described as impairments in communicative behaviour, interactions and social skills, and an 'inability to relate to people in an ordinary way.' 'Obsessive insistence on sameness' – Kanner felt this went to a deeper level than just a need for routine, and included symptoms such as repetitiveness, rigidity, single mindedness, pedantry and the inability to judge the significance of subtle differences.

At around the same time as Kanner's work, Asperger (1944, cited in Frith, 2003: 9–10) also published research about a group of children psychologically similar to those Kanner had observed, although the children studied by Asperger were not as severely impaired as those of Kanner's study. Asperger noted some additional features of the children, particularly with relation to their appearance and non-verbal social skills, documenting 'there is a poverty of facial expression and gestures ... the children totally follow their own impulses, regardless of the demands of the environment ... they are simply not geared towards learning from adults or teachers' (Asperger, 1944, cited in Frith, 2003: 10).

A diagnosis of 'classic autism' usually refers to the original diagnostic criteria as described by Kanner, and often indicates additional learning disabilities in 40–55 per cent of people (Chakrabarti and Fombonne, 2001). Autism is classified as a pervasive developmental disorder within the DSM-IV (American Psychiatric Association, 1994).

The deficits highlighted by Kanner and Asperger have been more recently described as 'the triad of impairments' following work by Wing and Gould (1979). This is now a commonly used descriptor for the deficits in social interaction, communication skills and imaginative play that define ASD as a disorder. It is of note that the triad of impairments focuses very specifically on impairments in 'social' communication, rather than viewing communication as a whole, general entity.

The emphasis is on the lack of ability and understanding socially, rather than an inability to communicate at all. The ability to communicate in a functional capacity (for example, requesting a drink, or the door to be open) often appears to be intact in people with ASD (Kaiser et al., 2001). Even with individuals who are unable to verbally communicate, there is evidence of an ability to communicate functionally (Tomasello and Camaioni, 1997; Sowden et al., 2008). Wing gives examples of non-verbal children with ASD showing a propensity to use other people as 'objects' in order to achieve need, for example: 'If they want something they cannot reach they grab you by the back of your hand or arm, not placing their hand inside yours or looking up at you, and pull you along to use your hand to reach the object they desire or to carry out an action for them such as turning the handle of a door' (Wing, 2002: 35).

The impairment in communication and social skills within ASD therefore seems to stem from a difficulty in using, interpreting and understanding the social aspects of communication, rather than specific difficulty in understanding the functional purpose of communication (Baron-Cohen and Bolton, 1993; Halle and Meadan, 2007).

The details of these impairments in social communication and interaction within ASD have been well chronicled. Children with ASD frequently avoid initiating or maintaining eye contact with others (Hutt and Ounsted, 1966, cited in Leekham and Hunnisett, 1998) and have difficulties following and monitoring gaze (Leekam and Hunnisett,1998), in giving, requesting and sharing information (Hurtig et al., 1982) and in conversational turn-taking (Prizant and Schuler, 1987). Deficits in imitation skills have also been demonstrated (Rogers and Pennington, 1991), in comprehension and expression of facial expressions (Sigman and Capps, 1997) and in use of gestures (Ohta, 1987).

Deficits in communication include lack of understanding of linguistic communication (for example, speech sounds, grammatical information and word meanings), paralinguistic communication (intonation, gesture and facial expression) and pragmatics (topic initiation, communicative intention and presupposition) (Landa, 2007). Infants with ASD can exhibit deficits in social and communication skills as early as the first year of life, for example, in the sharing of affective expression (Trevarthen and Daniel, 2005) and the use of gestures and responsiveness to others (Baranek, 1999). These deficits become more pronounced in later childhood (Wetherby et al., 1998, 2004), particularly in the areas of initiation of social communicative acts such as showing and joint attention (Baron-Cohen, 1989b; Wetherby et al., 1998).

Individuals with autistic spectrum disorder therefore have, by definition, impairments in social interaction and communication skills. While it is possible to teach individuals with ASD practical and self-help skills (National Research Council, 2001), the development of social communication and interaction skills is much more difficult to achieve and maintain (Murphy et al., 2005). Longitudinal studies of cohorts with ASD show that skills in the areas of communication and social interaction are least likely to improve or even, in some cases, be maintained (Beadle-Brown et al., 2006).

In the 1980s, theories surrounding 'theory of mind' in people who have autism became prominent. 'Theory of mind' is usually depicted as the ability to understand the knowledge, motives and actions of others, and is commonly assessed using experiments where individuals are asked to predict the thoughts and actions of actors in specific situations. Baron-Cohen (1997) suggests that 'theory of mind' is the way in which human beings relate, converse and socialise – including the general ability to interpret and react to a wealth of subtle social cues and situations. Baron-Cohen (1989a, 1995) and Frith and Happe (1994) demonstrated that children with ASD had difficulty with tasks and activities which required them to be able to see the viewpoint of others. Baron-Cohen called this deficit 'mind-blindness'.

Mind-blindness has implications for the whole symphony of communicative performance. In order to be able to communicate socially, certain flexible facilities are vital. This could include knowledge about and interpretation of, the person with whom you are communicating. For example the person's likes, interests or dislikes; your perception of their understanding of a subject; interpretation of their state of mind moment by moment together with the flow of their feelings and emotional state. Additionally, the ability to modify and alter communicative style based on this feedback in order to make it accessible and interesting to the other person is critical. Without this knowledge or ability to make insights or 'mindread' social conversations will be adversely affected.

Furthermore, Frith and Hill (2003) make the point that the effects of mind-blindness can extend to difficulty, sometimes extreme difficulty, in reading the detail of non-verbal communications. This can include difficulties in using and understanding non-verbal paralinguistic communication such as gesture (Mundy et al., 1993), eye contact and eye gaze (Koegel et al., 2009) and facial expression (Wallace et al., 2008).

This focus on non-verbal impairments has more recently moved to addressing what Lakin (2006) describes as 'automatic non-verbal communication'; that is, the exchange of the myriad of facial and other non-verbal signals that takes place on a non-conscious but still effective level between people communicating. Attention is now being given to the possible impairment of neurological factors such as mirror neurons in automatic processes (see McIntosh et al., 2006). My professional view at this time is that these trends towards greater focus in these areas are beginning to address the triad in more depth, and are bringing a greater understanding of the complexity of impairment in autism. More pertinently, the findings of neurological research are beginning to reflect the 'gut feeling' nature of Intensive Interaction. Practice that was initially led by empathy and instinct is now being supported by neurological reality.

Surely all of us involved – parents, carers, teachers and support assistants – share a frustration and bewilderment at the prospect of trying to nurture social interaction and communication with individuals with autism. Our current knowledge of the triad of impairments and its impact upon social and communicative skills not only emphasises the severity of difficulty in these areas, but must also impact upon how we enable these skills to be acquired.

The National Research Council (2001: 40) suggested that educational goals for students with ASD and additional learning difficulties often need to address language, social and adaptive skills that are not part of standard curricula. As I started out as a teacher of young people with ASD, I was intrigued by the reality of the central effects of the triad on the individuals with whom I was working. It seemed obvious to me that working with Intensive Interaction focused strongly on the communicative and social nature of their impairments, and utilised existing communicative actions of the students. The other popular approaches I observed in use did not achieve this, nor hold the power to create engaging interactions with them.

The fundamentals of communication and what is taught/enhanced through the use of Intensive Interaction

My understanding of the way the processes in Intensive Interaction, in particular the fundamentals of communication, relate to the triad of impairments in ASD form this section.

The link between the outcomes of Intensive Interaction activities and the potential impact of these outcomes upon the triad of impairments is not in any way radical or improbable. However, I feel that this link is not acknowledged, nor indeed even recognised, by many people working within the field of ASD. To me, Intensive Interaction seems a logical and obvious approach to fostering and developing communicative and social abilities in a learner-led, naturalistic way. It also addresses these issues with more depth and richness than any of the other currently used ASD approaches, focusing on areas of communicative development which are not often attended to by the more structured, teacher-led methods.

The 'fundamentals of communication' (FOC) (Nind and Hewett, 1994) is the name given to the description of social, communicative and interaction skills that are developed through the use of Intensive Interaction. The FOC are well described within the Intensive Interaction literature (Firth 2010; Firth and Barber, 2011; Hewett, this volume, Chapter 9; Nind and Hewett, 1994, 2001, 2005) and are based on the descriptions of outcomes within research on early infant–caregiver interactions. These 'fundamentals' form the basis of all subsequent social skills, and potentially, all subsequent learning (Hewett, this volume Chapter 9). The FOC can be defined as addressing the objectives described below, although this list is by no means exhaustive:

- learning to give brief attention to another person
- to share attention with another person
- learning to extend those attentions, learning to concentrate on another person
- developing shared attention into 'activities'
- taking turns in exchanges of behaviour
- to have fun, to play
- using and understanding eye contacts

- using and understanding facial expressions

- using and understanding non-verbal communication such as gesture and body language

- learning and understanding the use of physical contact

- learning, using and understanding vocalisations, having more varied and extensive vocalisations, gradually leading to more precise and meaningful vocalisations

- the possible formation of neural links.

The learning attainments within the fundamentals of communication focus on many of the areas of communication and/or social communication deficit and impairment described within the triad. Whether intentionally or inadvertently, Intensive Interaction seems to be an approach refined to the complexity of the communication impairments described in the triad. This does not imply in any sense that the approach is a panacea for autism, but that it is well focused in its outcomes upon the effects of some of the major impairments.

How the FOC work alongside the triad of impairments

As previously observed, Intensive Interaction was not developed as an ASD-specific approach. The initial group of learners who accessed Intensive Interaction were a group of adults representative of the range of impairments in learning difficulty. Dave Hewett and Melanie Nind make the point however that many (Nind and Powell, 2000), potentially more than half (discussion with Dave Hewett), had a diagnosis of ASD, and that there 'are many senses in which during its long development, Intensive Interaction became beautifully tailored to the learning and lifestyle needs of people on the spectrum' (Hewett, this volume, Chapter 9).

Subsequent to Nind and Hewett's early work, studies of Intensive Interaction have demonstrated increases in early social skills like smiling, engaging with others, and interactive games (Nind, 1993, cited in Kellett and Nind, 2003: 15). Kellett (2001, cited in Kellett and Nind, 2003: 16) reports increases in interactive social behaviour, and levels of engagement, following the implementation of Intensive Interaction for students with Profound and Multiple Learning Difficulties (PMLD) and autism. 'For those students who have not yet learned the fundamentals of early social communication, developing sociability and communication is an essential first step in their learning. Without it learning cannot become meaningful. Intensive Interaction is one approach within the umbrella of interactive pedagogy that has shown to be particularly successful' (Kellett and Nind, 2003: 185).

Peeters and Powell (2000) suggest that the responses given by the interactive partners during Intensive Interaction sessions assign social meaning to the learners' own behaviours. This interpretation of social significance or 'imputing' of meaning (Nind and Hewett, 2005) by the adult interactive partner also enables the learner to interact without having to adapt their own communication style. The learner is enabled to have a meaningful role within an interaction, without the pressure to communicate in a 'typical' way (Nind and Powell, 2000). Given the atypical communicative actions and responses often witnessed in people with ASD (Cox and Mesibov, 1995; Frith, 1991) it seems fitting to utilise an approach which accepts other, often idiosyncratic forms of communication, as social and meaningful in intent.

Imitation is accepted to be the single most frequently seen type of teacher responsiveness within Intensive Interaction activities (Nind and Hewett, 1994; Nind and Powell, 2000). I have found imitation to be a starting point to develop awareness of self and others, and to demonstrate to the learner that they can have control over others. The use of imitation with children with ASD has been found to increase social behaviours (Landa, 2007; Nadel et al., 1999). Imitation from an adult can increase eye contact, gesture and touching in children with ASD, as long as it is child led (Wimpory et al., 2007). Comparisons of imitative child-led and adult-led teaching strategies demonstrated that the child-led strategy resulted in a greater improvement in gaze, turn-taking, object use and joint attention when compared to the adult-led approach (Lewy and Dawson, 1992).

The Intensive Interaction practitioner holds back with their behaviour in order to let the other person largely lead the experience with their behaviour. Initiation of communication has been found to be a significant aspect of early communication learning by other researchers. Koegel et al. (1999) found that increasing initiating communication skills with children with ASD has a positive influence on other areas of communication. This is supported by the research of the National Research Council (2001) which suggests that interactive styles of teaching which offer initiation of communication activities have more beneficial long-term effects on the progress of children with ASD. From an Intensive Interaction practitioner's viewpoint, it is gratifying to take part in something which allows a realisation on the learner's behalf that they are in charge and can influence the whole procedure. I find that this 'eureka' moment is often the drive behind subsequent sessions, and motivates the learner into further interactions.

Intensive Interaction has a positive history of viewing stereotypical behaviours as having potentially communicative functions. This standpoint is further endorsed by the work of Durand and Merges (2001, cited in Smidt et al., 2007) and Nind and Kellett (2002). By joining in with these behaviours (as is the case in Intensive Interaction) we are communicating about the individual's choice of activity. It is plausible that the introduction of Intensive Interaction makes a positive contribution towards the students developing alternative behavioural repertoires. Barber (2007), who suggests that the imitation of stereotyped behaviours forms a 'common ground' for communication and interaction, also supports this viewpoint. An alternative view is that as the individual becomes more confident in communication and social interaction, and uses a wider range of skills in these areas, so people begin to respond in a more positive way, therefore increasing the likelihood of positive interactions, and reducing the incidences of challenging behaviours (Hewett, 1996).

The processes of a typical Intensive Interaction activity can be seen to be supportive for and sensitive to learners who may be experiencing extreme anxiety and/or social confusion as a norm of everyday life. There are some key features which establish this: the child-led, child-centred principle, the preparedness of the teacher to be responsive and to pause in order to allow the learner to be in the lead, and the core issue of the flow of the activity developing from the responsiveness of the teacher to the actions of the learner. The lack of a required or specified outcome, or 'tasklessness' (Nind and Hewett, 1994) of the teacher within these activities, results in a relaxed and undemanding communicative exchange, which, in my experience, must inevitably contribute to a lowering of anxiety for the learner. Within my own practice of Intensive Interaction I have noted the impact on the learner of 'tasklessness'. That sudden fear of being required to do something disappears, and the interactive exchange flows without interruption or trepidation.

Central too then, surely, is the 'tuned-inness' of the teacher to all feedback from the learner throughout the flow of the activity. This is emphasised in all Intensive Interaction literature (for example, see Nind and Hewett 1994, 2005; Nind and Powell, 2000). This central operational principle would seem to do two highly beneficial things. First, it ensures that the sensibilities of the person with ASD are taken fully into account during every passing moment. Thus, all things being equal, the learner is receiving a customised, synchronised and fully sensitised communication experience moment by moment – the 'good fit' between the teacher's input and the learner's needs (Hewett and Nind, 1998). Secondly, the often idiosyncratic behaviour of the learner is read and used communicatively, as a result of the highly tuned-in, sensitive approach being utilised by the teacher.

There is also the manner in which the continuous process of dynamic activities furnishes the learner with rich, naturalistic, structured and repetitive learning opportunities to hone and enhance these understandings and performances (Hewett, this volume, Chapter 9; Hewett and Nind, 1998). The complexity of, for instance, non-verbal communication learning seems to demand a social ecology that is flexible, supportive and, yes, dynamic and repetitive. This repetitiveness is also a major component of the structure – a feature of activities that is so frequently held to be vital for people with ASD.

However, it is also worth noting that while the processes within Intensive Interaction can be predictable and repetitive, this is not always the case. The development and expansion of the learning attainments can result in more complex and unexpected activities. In many ways Intensive Interaction can almost take the form of a 'trial and error' approach, as both partners within the interaction become more confident and explorative. Some of the most exciting and successful-seeming interactions I have taken part in have been the result of an unanticipated alteration within a familiar interactive repertoire. Perhaps the security of these familiar activities allows change and adaptation to be less threatening, thus enabling greater exploration of social and communicative skills.

The intricate relationship between the FOC and the triad of impairments, therefore, is one which can be analysed, explored and ultimately, in my opinion, justified in terms of the impact of Intensive Interaction activities upon the social and communication difficulties within ASD. The impact of this within the field of special education should be more acutely realised than it currently is. For whatever reason, while the developmental, learner-led ethos of Intensive Interaction is frequently lauded, it often does not seem to translate into general practice in services. In particular, the domain of ASD specific approaches has seemed more reticent to embrace the development of communication within this type of naturalistic framework.

Resolution

Part of my motivation for writing this paper is to address the gap between commonplace practice in the field of ASD and the outcomes of studies such as the already cited National Research Council (2001). They indicate that approaches for teaching skills in social communication and interaction which are naturalistic, developmentally appropriate and child-led have the most success in regards to development in these areas (Charman, 2010; Greenspan and Wieder, 1997).

I would not claim that this chapter makes points that are in any way revelatory. However, the nature of what seems to be common practice and approaches suggest that these points still need to be stated clearly in such opportunities as this volume. This orientation to a naturalistic model based on developmental appropriateness was richly argued as far back as 1986 (Dawson and Galpert, 1986), and has continued to feature in special education literature (Charman, 2010; Greenspan and Wieder, 1997; Klinger and Dawson, 1992, cited in National Research Council, 2001; Koegel et al., 1998). The nature of Intensive Interaction ensures that these attainments are repeatedly practiced and consolidated in a naturalistic way, and the myriad of learning experiences which take place within these sessions cannot be measured quantitatively.

However, much of the current practice in the field of autism-specific approaches seems to focus on a rigid, highly structured way of teaching and assessing these very complex, sophisticated and, at times, surprisingly diverse skills. Furthermore, many of the current approaches (Treatment and Education of Autistic and Related Communication-handicapped Children (TEACCH), Checklist for Autism in Toddlers (CHAT) and Picture Exchange Communication System (PECS)) do not even appear to address the social communication difficulties, focusing instead on functional communication skills. The danger lies in trying to quantify and formalise these social communication attainments into a check list or regulated set of skills to be worked through. The learning of social communication skills is too intricate to be broken down in this manner.

For me, one of the most startling outcomes of using Intensive Interaction with learners with ASD has been the consolidation and extension of these attainments. I could never have predicted the ways in which my students began to adapt and broaden their learning to other situations, people and even, in some cases, each other. I think this demonstrates the richness of the learning process within

Intensive Interaction, and also the peril of trying to formalise these learning outcomes. If we cannot predict the effects of the development of social and communicative competency, how can we accurately quantify it?

Above all, Intensive Interaction allows the development of the messy, jumbled and unique process of learning to communicate and socialise, without placing demands or restrictions upon the learners. Surely this is the best possible way to foster the development of something as unique, complex and ultimately vital, as the ability to communicate and socialise with those around us.

Enabling the exploration and development of the fundamentals of social communication in a relaxed, pleasurable and responsive manner, is possibly the most precious experience we, as educators, can give to the young people with whom we work. The challenge is to recognise, facilitate and value these essential moments of interaction, through the creation of a culture and ethos of communication, in which Intensive Interaction is a fundamental component.

☐ Summary

I have attempted to highlight and explore the key relationship between the triad of impairments and Intensive Interaction. My intention has been to emphasise the importance of using Intensive Interaction to develop attainments which we know can be lacking in individuals with ASD, and highlight the potential facility of this approach for addressing those needs. More importantly, I hope to have addressed the significance of teaching and learning these things, especially for people who are often considered as incapable or uninterested in social interaction. Just because someone does not socially communicate in a traditional manner, it does not indicate that social interaction is unwelcome or unwanted. *Our* skills should lie in our ability to interpret and act upon these behaviours in order to enable social interaction to take place meaningfully.

References

American Psychiatric Association (1994) *Diagnostic and Statistical Manual of Mental Disorders*, 4th edn. Washington, DC: American Psychiatric Association.

Baranek, G.T. (1999) 'Autism during infancy: a retrospective video analysis of sensory-motor and social behaviours at 9–12 months of age', *Journal of Autism and Developmental Disorders*, 29: 213–24.

Barber, M. (2007) 'Imitation, interaction and dialogue using Intensive Interaction: tea party rules', *Support for Learning*, 22(3): 124–30.

Baron-Cohen, S. (1989a) 'The autistic child's theory of mind: a case of specific developmental delay', *Journal of Child Psychology and Psychiatry*, 30: 285–97.

Baron-Cohen, S. (1989b) 'Perceptual role taking and protodeclarative pointing in autism', *British Journal of Developmental Psychology*, 7: 113–27.

Baron-Cohen, S. (1995) *Mindblindess*. Cambridge, MA: MIT Press.

Baron-Cohen, S. (1997) *The Mal-adapted Mind: Classical Readings in Evolutionary Psychopathology*. Hove: Psychology Press.

Baron-Cohen, S. and Bolton, P. (1993) *Autism: The Facts*. Oxford: Oxford University Press.

Beadle-Brown, J., Murphy, G. and Wing, L. (2006) 'The Camberwell Cohort 25 years on: characteristics and changes in skills over time', *Journal of Applied Research in Intellectual Disabilities*, 19: 317–29.

Chakrabarti, S. and Fombonne, E. (2001) 'Pervasive developmental disorders in preschool children', *Journal of the American Medical Association*, 285: 3093–9.

Charman, T. (2010) 'Developmental approaches to understanding and treating autism', *Folia Phoniatrica et Logopaedica*, 62(4): 166–77.

Cox, R.D. and Mesibov, G. (1995) 'Relationship between autism and learning disabilities', in E. Schopler and G.B. Mesibov (eds), *Learning and Cognition in Autism: Current Issues in Autism*. New York: Plenum Press.

Dawson, G. and Galpert, L. (1986) 'A developmental model for facilitating the social behavior of autistic children', in E. Schopler and G.B. Mesibov (eds), *Social Behaviour in Autism*. New York: Plenum Press.

Firth, G. (2010) 'Issues associated with human communication', in G. Firth, R. Berry and C. Irvine (eds), *Understanding Intensive Interaction*. London: Jessica Kingsley.

Firth, G. and Barber, M. (2011) *Using Intensive Interaction with a Person with a Social or Communicative Impairment*. London: Jessica Kingsley.

Frith, U. (1991) *Autism and Asperger Syndrome*. Cambridge: Cambridge University Press.

Frith, U. (2003) *Autism: Explaining the Enigma*, 2nd edn. Oxford: Blackwell Publishing.

Frith, U. and Happe, F. (1994) 'Autism: beyond theory of mind', *Cognition*, 50: 115–32.

Frith, U. and Hill, E.L. (2003) 'Autism: mind and brain', *Philosophical Transactions of The Royal Society*, Series B, 358: 277–80.

Greenspan, S.I. and Wieder, S. (1997) 'Developmental patterns and outcomes in infants and children with disorders in relating and communicating: a chart review of 200 cases of children with autistic spectrum diagnoses', *Journal of Developmental and Learning Disorders*, 1: 87–141.

Halle, J. and Meadan, H. (2007) 'A protocol for assessing early communication of young children with autism and other developmental disabilities', *Topics in Early Childhood Special Education*, 27(1): 49–61.

Hewett, D. (1996) 'How to do Intensive Interaction', in M. Collis and P. Lacey (eds), *Interactive Approaches to Teaching: A Framework for INSET.* London: David Fulton.

Hewett, D. and Nind, M. (eds) (1998) *Interaction in Action: Reflections on the Use of Intensive Interaction.* London: David Fulton.

Kaiser, A.P., Hester, P.P. and McDuffie, A.S. (2001) 'Supporting communication in young children with developmental disabilities', *Mental Retardation and Developmental Disabilities Research Reviews*, 7: 143–50.

Kellett, M. and Nind, M. (2003) *Implementing Intensive Interaction in Schools: Guidance for Practitioners, Managers and Co-ordinators.* London: David Fulton.

Koegel, L.K., Koegel, R.L., Shoshan, Y. and McNerney, E. (1999) 'Pivotal response intervention II: preliminary long-term outcome data', *The Journal of the Association for Persons with Severe Handicaps*, 24(3): 186–98.

Koegel, R.L., Camarata, S., Koegel, L.K., Ben-Tall, A. and Smith, A.E. (1998) 'Increasing speech intelligibility in children with autism', *Journal of Autism and Developmental Disorders*, 28(3): 241–51.

Koegel, R.L., Vernon, T.W. and Koegel, L.K. (2009) 'Improving social initiations in young children with autism using reinforcers with embedded social interactions', *Journal of Autism & Developmental Disorders*, 39(9): 1240–51.

Lakin, J.L. (2006) 'Automatic cognitive processes and nonverbal communication', in V. Manusov and M.L. Patterson (eds), *The Sage Handbook of Nonverbal Communication.* Thousand Oaks, CA: Sage.

Landa, R. (2007) 'Early communication development and intervention for children with autism', *Mental Retardation and Developmental Disabilities Research Reviews*, 13: 16–25.

Leekam, S.R and Hunnisett, E. (1998) 'Targets and cues: gaze-following in children with autism', *Journal of Child Psychology and Psychiatry and Allied Disciplines*, 39(7): 951–63.

Lewy, A.L. and Dawson, G. (1992) 'Social stimulation and joint attention in young autistic children', *Journal of Abnormal Child Psychology*, 20(6): 555–66.

McIntosh, D.N., Reichmann-Decker, A., Winkielman, P. and Wilbarger, J.L. (2006) 'When the social mirror breaks: deficits in automatic, but not voluntary, mimicry of emotional facial expression in autism', *Developmental Science*, 9(3): 295–302.

Mundy, P., Sigman, M. and Kasari, C. (1993) 'The theory of mind and joint attention in autism', in S. Baron-Cohen, H. Tager-Flusberg and D. Cohen (eds), *Understanding Other Minds: Perspectives from Autism*, Oxford: Oxford University Press.

Murphy, G.H., Beadle-Brown, J., Wing, L., Gould, J., Shah, A. and Holmes, N. (2005) 'Chronicity of challenging behaviours in people with severe intellectual disabilities and/or autism: a total population sample', *Journal of Autism and Developmental Disorder*, 35(4): 405–18

Nadel, J., Guerini, C., Peze, A. and Rivet, C. (1999) 'The evolving nature of imitation as a format for communication', in J. Nadel and G. Butterworth (eds), *Imitation in Infancy.* Cambridge: Cambridge University Press.

National Research Council (2001) *Educating Children with Autism.* Washington, DC: National Academy Press.

Nind, M. and Hewett, D. (1994) *Access to Communication: Developing the Basics of Communication in People with Severe Learning Difficulties through Intensive Interaction.* London: David Fulton.

Nind, M. and Hewett, D. (2001) *A Practical Guide to Intensive Interaction.* Kidderminster: British Institute of Learning Disabilities.

Nind, M. and Hewett, D. (2005) *Access to Communication: Developing the Basics of Communication with People with Severe Learning Difficulties through Intensive Interaction,* 2nd edn. London: David Fulton.

Nind, M. and Kellett, M. (2002) 'Responding to individuals with severe learning difficulties and stereotyped behaviour: challenges for an inclusive era', *European Journal of Special Needs Education,* 17(3): 265–82.

Nind, M. and Powell, S. (2000) 'Intensive interaction and autism: some theoretical concerns', *Children and Society,* 14: 98–109.

Ohta, M. (1987) 'Cognitive disorders of infantile autism: a study of employing WISC, spatial relationship conceptualization and gesture imitations', *Journal of Autism and Developmental Disorders,* 17(1): 45–62.

Peeters, T. and Powell, S. (2000) 'Intensive Interaction and Children with Autism', in S. Powell (ed.), *Helping Children with Autism to Learn.* London: David Fulton.

Prizant, B. and Schuler, A. (1987) *Handbook of Autism and Pervasive Developmental Disorders.* New York: Wiley.

Rogers, S.J. and Pennington, B.F. (1991) 'A theoretical approach to the deficits in infantile autism', *Development and Psychopathology,* 3: 137–62.

Sigman, M. and Capps, L. (1997) *Children with Autism: A Developmental Perspective.* Cambridge, MA: Harvard University Press.

Smidt, A., Balandin, S., Reed, V. and Sigafoos, J. (2007) 'A communication training programme for residential staff working with adults with challenging behaviour: pilot data on intervention effects', *Journal of Applied Research in Intellectual Disability,* 20: 16–29.

Sowden, H., Perkins, M. and Clegg, J. (2008) 'The co-development of speech and gesture in children with autism', *Clinical Linguistics and Phonetics,* 22(10): 804–13.

Tomasello, M. and Camaioni, L. (1997) 'A comparison of the gestural communication of apes and human infants', *Human Development,* 40: 7–24.

Trevarthen, C. and Daniel, S. (2005) 'Disorganised rhythm and synchrony: early signs of autism and Rett syndrome', *Brain Development,* 27: 25–34.

Wallace, S., Coleman, M. and Bailey, A. (2008) 'An investigation of basic facial expression recognition in autism spectrum disorders', *Cognition & Emotion,* 22(7): 1353–80.

Wetherby, A., Prizant, B. and Hutchinson, T. (1998) 'Communicative, social/affective and symbolic profiles of young children with autism and pervasive developmental disorders', *American Journal of Speech and Language Pathology,* 7: 79–91.

Wetherby, A., Woods, J. and Allen, L. (2004) 'Early indicators of autism spectrum disorders in the second year of life', *Journal of Autism and Developmental Disorders*, 34: 473–93.

Wimpory, D.C., Hobson, R.P. and Nash, S. (2007) 'What facilitates social engagement in preschool children with autism?', *Journal of Autism and Developmental Disorders*, 37: 564–73.

Wing, L. (2002) *The Autistic Spectrum*. London: Constable and Robinson.

Wing, L. and Gould, J. (1979) 'Severe impairments of social interaction and associated abnormalities in children: epidemiology and classification', *Journal of Autism and Developmental Disorders*, 9: 11–29.

6

Promoting communication rather than generating data

Mark Barber

Chapter overview

This chapter was prompted by the perception that teachers and therapists working with learners with profound intellectual and multiple disabilities (PIMD) in educational and social settings are feeling increasingly pressurised into jettisoning person-centred interactive teaching approaches in favour of teaching to accommodate documentation. While 'administrivia' (Rice, 2009) has increased its demands on the productive time of teachers and allied health professionals, it also seems that in the last decade there has been an equally daunting increase in the presence of commercially packaged intervention resources, which reflect a product management ethos to teaching, projecting and achieving outcomes under the guise of accountability.

In the light of this perceived pressure, this chapter considers perspectives of how to best support learners with complex intellectual disabilities to acquire the vital successful communicative experiences which form the essential platform for future social functioning. It will acquaint or reacquaint readers with some of the attributes that indicate Intensive Interaction as a principled, realistic and valuable approach to supporting learners to acquire successful experience of communication and social interaction.

Finally there is a description of a method of achieving rigorous and accountable recognition of measurable changes in learning and involvement in the process of communication. This method is currently being used in many special educational settings in Australia and New Zealand.

Recipes for intervention

We live in a professional climate which often pressurises practitioners into accounting for their time and energies in terms of results achieved. The need to demonstrate progress and effective interventions often leads teachers, therapists and health professionals working with students and clients who experience PIMD to view supporting communication in terms of achieving predefined outcomes or attaching relative values to the learner's communicative attempts. However, many of the critical aspects of communication development are difficult to record while others are likely to be absent from checklists of prescribed indicators.

There is a subtle attraction for teachers and therapists to go about the business of promoting communication with people who have profound intellectual disabilities by following the conveniently linear hierarchies that characterise the predominantly assessment-based resources, which are commercially available. One of the main temptations of these resources appears to be that the orderly manner in which the assessment elements are mapped out suggests a logical 'recipe' for intervention which corresponds conveniently with an outcomes-based style of teaching. Thus practitioners are provided with a framework of notionally predictable goals to aim for and structure their teaching, which in turn generate finite outcomes that conform to the need for observable and measurable data. This is in spite of the fact that communication is much more than simply directing others. Nind and Hewett (2001) comment that much of what we talk about to each other is simply the 'hot air' of companionship. Mostly, most of us simply like to be with other people and enjoy each other, laugh, be companions.

Styles of intervention that emphasise outcome over process, which is less easily observed, subtly invite practitioners to assume that learning is occurring because of the performance of communication. However, communication is more than a performance, it involves understanding of and involvement in a process. At very early levels of social understanding, especially in the context of intellectually disabled learners, communication and social interaction might simply involve degrees of mutual adjustment. For those working with people experiencing PIMD, successful interaction often depends on their familiarity, observation and the inferences made about the learner's 'pre or proto-symbolic utterances, bodily movements, changes in muscle tone and other subtle cues' (Hostyn and Maes, 2009). While evidence of progress, change or elaboration of these responses can be identified, the manner in which individual learners will express their increased involvement simply cannot be predicted. The inherent complexity of the communicative process makes it difficult to construct predictive goals about social and communication learning outcomes with these learners. Indeed, doing so inevitably leads to strategies being framed on the basis of what the teacher, therapist or system wants rather than how the learner senses and perceives or learns about their world.

Roles and outcomes

Communication is not a performance that can be task analysed and taught in a linear fashion; it is a social process that is learned through involvement and enjoyment. This section examines the contradictions inherent in interventions based on manufactured transactions using symbols, with the goal that these pragmatic exchanges will eventually result in the use of more socially complex communicative functions.

Rather than using explicit teaching methods based on the transition of information and the direct teaching of skills, the teacher's role might be seen as one which creates learning situations which provide opportunities to solve real problems (Westwood, 2001). The nature of the learning situations created by professionals will to some extent depend on their perception of the most effective style of intervention, as well as how they perceive the role they have as the 'skilled partner' in the process of assisting a learner to acquire successful communicative experience. Interviewing staff in adult disability settings about their perceptions of their roles, Clegg et al. (1996) identified two main camps: *providers* who engaged in predominantly instrumental relationships based on meeting needs and *meaning-makers* who considered their role was to understand their client's moods and gestures and to try to create meaning within a relationship with them. It is speculated here that teachers and therapists are more than likely to fall more or less within these roles as well.

Considerations for 'providers' of communicative outcomes

The majority of communication interventions by professionals with learners at very early stages of communication are focused on providing the learner with the means to express needs and wants (Light et al., 2002) and, by inference, requests. In spite of concerns resulting from the nature and use of behaviourist methods (see, for example, Collis and Lacey, 1996), the assessment and teaching of complex areas of early development has been and is still heavily influenced by behaviourist thinking (CCEA, 2009). The focus on teaching request functions that characterise many of these interventions, reflects an emphasis on observable behavioural responses to demonstrate learning. This leads many teachers and therapists to place a higher value on extrinsic outcomes in communicative performance rather than purposeful involvement in the process of communication. There is also an inherent lack of appreciation about the forms, function and developmental pathway of human communication development.

While the motives of these interventions are not in question, such approaches suggest an implicit expectation that skills acquired in controlled settings will be generalised to the more fluid and everyday experience of communication. The dominant presence that requesting and indicating have in these styles of intervention also promotes the assumption that they must be the most important functions of communication. It is undeniably important for learners to gain the skills to request and indicate preferences, however, in the words of the mother described by Light et al. (2002: 187), 'there's more to life than cookies'.

The use of visual symbols to elicit request responses from students with PIMD can seem a common activity in special educational settings. Teachers and therapists construct teaching contexts in which the learner will be most likely to indicate their desire for a specific response or reward. The intervention is intended to largely reflect the early proto-imperative signalling behaviours seen in typical development, when young communicators coordinate their attention on the 'listener' and on the object they want them to act on. This approach to promoting communication invites the belief that the most motivating aspect of communication is the control over the environment that such request functions give the learner, while utilising the operant mechanism of an immediate and reinforcing environmental response to an action.

The use of symbols and pictographs to augment the communication of learners who already demonstrate symbol use is a logical and well-established practice. However, the increasingly common use of this intervention with pre-symbolic and even communicatively pre-intentional learners must be questioned. Even as a 'least-worst' intervention or one that immerses the learner in a facsimile of an exchange, there are substantial grounds for concern while there are certainly more enriching communicative experiences open to these learners.

Proto-imperative signalling can be equated with a communicational version of 'tool use' in typical development, where the caregiver is the tool. The child coordinates person-directed and object-directed actions, engaging the adult to obtain a desired object. Increasingly attuned caregivers act on the combination of inferred meanings from their child's visual behaviours and gestures, contextual cues and the child's actual behaviour, leading the child to begin to recognise the caregiver's responsiveness. Whatever the underpinning mechanism, the child's nascent realisation of 'means–ends' relationships between actions and consequences leads them to begin to indicate the focus of their attention to the adult.

In typical development, following the acquisition of a critical mass of successful experience (Barber, 2000) in a range of cognitive and communicative functions, proto-imperative signalling gives way to proto-declarative initiations, where the child draws the attention of the 'listener' to an object for the purpose of joint attention. Here, the more complex function of initiation is not to have the listener act as a means to an end, but to change the focus of attention of the listener (Stephenson and Lightfoot, 1996).

In Camaioni's (1993) view, cited in Stephenson and Lightfoot (1996: 150), while development of proto-imperatives is a step towards intentional communication, intent 'is only truly present when the child coordinates object-directed and person-directed actions to alter the focus of the listener's attention and interest'. They opine that in the context of severe intellectual disability, the transition phase which separates pre-intention from communicative intention occurs between the emergence of proto-imperatives and the beginning of proto-declaratives.

Based on the work of Bates et al. (1979) and others, Stephenson and Lightfoot (1996: 153) suggested that the use of symbols 'emerge only after proto-declaratives are established'. Carter and Iacono (2002) confirm this order of emergence in typical development, finding that frequent production of intentional communicative acts appears to precede the emergence of symbolic communication. The inescapable suggestion is that the cognitive architecture that supports learners to recognise the relationship between a sign and the 'something else' it represents is only present following the considerable cognitive elaborations that underlie the conceptual leap from proto-imperative signalling to frequent intentional acts. In other words, considerable experience in the processes of being a communicator is necessary in order to develop the cognitive structures that support the application of communication to more extrinsic outcomes.

Thus, the expectation that pre-symbolic learners with severe or profound intellectual disabilities will learn to use pictographs with understanding is questioned. However, it is accepted that these learners can and frequently do demonstrate the ability to acquire the behaviours associated with achieving an available reinforcer.

Continued consideration of interventions based on symbol use with these learners highlights further problematic issues and perceptions. Typically, very early signalling in socially responsive settings provides the learner with increasingly successful means–ends experience of achieving desired outcomes. Early examples of these indicating behaviours typically involve vocalising and reaches, which do not require the learner to alternate their glance between the object and the adult. Indeed, Harding (1984) reported that the vocal behaviours directed at desired items actually emerged in many infants before the understanding that another person needed to be present for the signal to work. Learning acquired from the responses of those who happily *are* present, to their youngster's effortful contributions, can be speculated to support the process of eventual emergence of proto-imperatives that use consistent alternating glance.

In request situations where the learner coordinates the object and teacher or therapist with glance behaviours, the process is a relatively simple one involving glances between two venues – that is, the target item and the 'listener'. But the insertion of a graphic symbol into the context adds an additional venue, which requires the learner to coordinate a triple focus of attention. For someone with a severe or profound intellectual disability this is likely to prove to be difficult, as it represents a much more complex problem.

By apparently simplifying a learning situation or communicative act by stripping it down to the level of what is observable, the meaning of the actions can be confused and the complex nature of the activity can be lost. For the teacher or therapist working in this context, there is also the potential complication of the 'confirmation bias' (Barber et al., 1995; Reason, 1990) which relates to the point in an activity where, having deployed a strategy, the person involved primarily seeks confirmatory evidence that the strategy they have chosen was the correct one, even in the face of evidence to the contrary. The teacher or therapist's focus on interpreting what is actually the learner's attempt to activate an available environmental reinforcer, as measurable evidence of communicative behaviour, might be interpreted as a strategy being primarily guided by this 'confirmation bias'.

'Interactions to express needs and wants focus not on the partner but, rather, on the target object or action. Once the object or action is attained ... the communication usually ends' (Light, 1988, cited in Light et al., 2002: 188). Interventions to elicit expressions of needs and wants are relatively straightforward and easy to implement (for example, Reichle et al., 1991) and to measure. Without doubt teachers, therapists and direct care workers who divide their time between the students and clients in their charge, consider themselves to be 'time poor'. Many clearly perceive that this type of intervention addresses several issues: purposeful teaching, obvious evidence, straightforward data. Indeed, as Light et al. (2002: 189–90) comment, 'interventions to build skills in expressing needs and wants have formed the centre piece of AAC (Augmentative and Alternative Communication) programmes for people who are beginning communicators'. Interventions to promote social closeness and interaction are certainly less straightforward and may be more complex to develop as they 'rely on participants being able to sustain the interaction through the active engagement or involvement of both participants' (Light et al., 2002: 190). Yet it is uncontroversial to say that while they are critical to emotional well-being and to the development of social understanding, opportunities to engage in and explore purely social interaction are sometimes counter to the expectations of employers (Forster and Iacono, 2008) and largely absent from the special education environment (for example, Hewett, 2007).

Making meaning in shared interaction – some considerations for practice

Interactive approaches to supporting the development of communication focus on providing the learner with the motivation and the skills to maintain their inclusion in social interactions, which are usually entered into for their own sake. Interactive styles of intervention focus on teaching through understanding and deem positive interactive relationships with others to be essential for the personal autonomy and identity of the learner, as well as for their emotional well-being. Central to this approach is the understanding that learning is contingent upon good interpersonal relationships and that interaction between learner and adult is vital in leading to cognitive change (Vygotsky, 1978). Understanding is developed through interactive relationships which foster negotiation, participation and motivation. Crucially, there is the recognition that 'teaching is not always dependent on dividing that which is to be taught into its constituent parts' (CCEA, 2009: 14).

A central principle in interactive approaches to teaching and learning and in Intensive Interaction is that communication is a dynamic process which cannot be divided into its component parts for the purposes of teaching, but must be supported within fluid and learner-led sequences of action learning. Whatever their contribution, the responses and adjustments that the learner makes within social encounters are seen as the visible signs of cognitive engagement in the communicative process.

The skilled partner does not limit their own responses to the learner's behaviours in favour of those which might approximate 'conventions' but supports the learner to explore the possibilities of interactive response. Indeed, with many learners, the success of an interaction is not dependant on their interactive skills at all, but on the ability of the 'skilled' partner to interpret and respond to any behaviour they demonstrate, in a manner which intrigues or invites their continued involvement. Influenced by Bruner's (1981: 160) observation of parents 'going to the level on which the child is operating, the approach sets out to support learners to explore playfully ritualised interactions and revisit what Bruner (1981) described as 'frames' as possible contexts for embellishment or elaboration of communicative skills. 'Essentially, Intensive Interaction teaches the communication learning that occurs prior to symbolic representation – that is the bulk of communication learning' (Hewett, 2007: 117).

The content of interactions follows the focus of the learner rather than any agenda or indicated goal of the skilled partner as this ensures that interactions are intrinsically motivating to the person doing the learning. In addition to the growing body of publications that support the use of Intensive Interaction, including the UK government (for example, DoH, 2009), precedent may be found in other investigations into essential elements in exemplary practice in the context of communication learning; 'the quality of [a learner's] attention is substantially greater when focussed on events of their own choosing, than to events chosen by someone else' (Warren and Yoder, 1998: 373). Light et al. (2002: 198–200) identify that best practice for interactions to promote social interaction should encourage caregivers to focus on the individual's interest, be of interest to the learner, be sustainable over multiple exchanges, involve reciprocal turn-taking by both participants, and allow the learner to participate in multiple ways using gross rather than discrete behaviours. In their 2009 review and analysis of literature relating to interaction with people experiencing PIMD included on ERIC, PsychINFO, and Social Sciences Citation Index, Hostyn and Maes identified a number of reoccurring themes that emerged as being important characteristics of interaction: *sensitive responsiveness* or the 'dyadic quality of the interaction' or 'the way partners perceive each other's signals ... and correspondingly respond to each other' (for example, Ainsworth et al., 1978 in Hostyn and Maes, 2009: 9); *joint attention* or 'congruence between the behaviours of the partners' and 'mutual agreements about what is to be communicated between partners, about when and how interactions take place and for how long' (Fogel, 1993 in Hostyn and Maes, 2009: 9); *co-regulation* (Olsson, 2004 in Hostyn and Maes, 2009: 9) where mutuality, reciprocity, mutual participation and turn-taking were grouped along with the important idea of attunement, where skilled partners behave with regard to the 'feeling state of the partner' during interactions; and, finally, the value of the emotional component.

Accountability

Dynamic styles of teaching communication do present some problems for professionals manoeuvring within the evidence-generating climate, which prevails on them to account for and measure progress or developments based on their choice of intervention. How does one accurately measure the degree of interest, or level of anticipation or affiliation that has been demonstrated in an interaction? When learning outcomes occur that are different to the specified indicators listed in the hierarchy used to structure teaching goals, are they less significant?

Typically, predictive goals are constructed by the teacher, therapist or key worker, often in collaboration with parents and carers, at the start of reporting cycles and evaluated prior to reporting phases of the institution involved. In nearly all settings, the actual judgements that constitute the evaluation (that is, did the learner achieve criteria of success?) is largely a solitary process, taken on by the person whose responsibility it is to write the goals.

When Intensive Interaction was introduced in Australia, a number of practices were developed to ensure that the levels of accountability used by involved schools were *more* rigorous than those standards used by teachers and others, working within the dominant culture of predictive behavioural goals.

In line with recommendations from a number of publications about Intensive Interaction (for example, Kellett and Nind, 2003; Nind and Hewett, 2001; Firth and Barber, 2010) the focus of accountability has been placed on *reporting on* instead of *predicting* learning. Practitioners indicate their intentions by writing a 'learning focus' which describes the types of learning opportunities that will be provided, along with the general tenet of the responses and levels of support that might be necessary. The three-part policy outlined in Kellett and Nind (2003: 146) provides staff with a conceptual framework for describing different perspectives of interaction, as well as giving a structure for them to consider when writing prose reports about the learning observed across the reporting cycle. Within these documents, equal value is placed on learning in informal settings (for example, recess, lulls in classroom routines) as that which occurs in more formal or timetabled settings. Recognising that 'for learners with profound intellectual disabilities, progression is not necessarily only movement up a hierarchical ladder of skills and knowledge' (QCA, 2001: 16), opportunities for interaction with a variety of partners are encouraged across the many interactive contexts available creating settings for lateral progress to be demonstrated.

Evidence gathering and analysis

As interaction does not generate collectable objective evidence per se, practitioners are recommended to collect video of interactions with each learner on a weekly basis. With the advances in handheld digital video camera technology since the turn of the century, it is possible to capture previously unheard of levels of information about 'what just happened'. Digital video allows infinite numbers of replays and analysis with the attraction of convenient storage of huge amounts of footage.

Practitioners are encouraged to record reflective, narrative accounts of their interactions, which include their impressions of what they considered to be significant or novel features of encounters. Although these accounts are clearly subjective they at least assist with the transfer of useful information between colleagues. At best they can be collated across a period to form a timeline which traces the emergence of new features within existing 'frames', or the frequency and rhythm with which the learners revisit familiar interactive territory.

The main purpose of collecting video evidence of interactions is to use it to assist in the recognition of progress over time. This process has been formalised in many settings in Australia and New Zealand by the practice of using the video as the basis of a group moderation process, which involves all of the staff using the approach in the particular setting and others who may be interested. In smaller settings where there may only be a handful of staff, this process has involved inter-school moderation.

The key document in the process of moderation is the 'Framework for Recognising Attainment' (Figure 6.1; QCA, 2001). This framework describes a spectrum of involvement, response and participation from 'encounter' to 'participation' and forms the structure within which vertical or lateral progress can be accounted for. The framework essentially forms the early levels of the performance descriptions or 'P levels' introduced by the document *Planning, Teaching and Assessing the Curriculum for Pupils with Learning Difficulties* (QCA, 2001).

A framework for recognising attainment	
Encounter	Pupils are present during an experience or activity without any obvious learning outcome, although for some pupils, *for example, those who withhold their attention or their presence from many situations*, their willingness to tolerate a shared activity may, in itself, be significant.
Awareness	Pupils appear to show awareness that something has happened and notice, fleetingly focus on or attend to an object, event or person, *for example, by briefly interrupting a pattern of self-absorbed movement or vocalisation.*
Attention and response	Pupils attend and begin to respond, often not consistently, to what is happening, *for example, by showing signs of surprise, enjoyment, frustration or dissatisfaction*, demonstrating the beginning of an ability to distinguish between different people, objects, events and places.
Engagement	Pupils show more consistent attention to, and can tell the difference between, specific events in their surroundings, *for example, by focused looking or listening; turning to locate objects, events or people; following moving objects and events through movements of their eyes, head or other body parts.*
Participation	Pupils engage in sharing, taking turns and the anticipation of familiar sequences of events, *for example, by smiling, vocalising or showing other signs of excitement*, although these responses may be supported by staff or other pupils.
Involvement	Pupils actively strive to reach out, join in or comment in some way on the activity itself or on the actions or responses of the other pupils, *for example, by making exploratory hand and arm movements, seeking eye contact with staff or other pupils, or by speaking, signing or gesturing.*
Gaining skills and understanding	Pupils gain, strengthen or make general use of their skills, knowledge, concepts or understanding that relate to their experience of the curriculum, *for example, they can recognise the features of an object and understand its relevance, significance and use.*

Figure 6.1 A framework for recognising attainment
Source: QCA (2001: 16)

Process

Towards the end of the establishment's reporting cycle, key workers for individual learners have the responsibility of finding at least one 10-minute period of recent video of the learner, which demonstrates what they believe to be the learner's most sophisticated level of inter-activity with a communicative partner. This footage is viewed (often several times) and forms the basis of a professional discussion among staff.

Although the student may have interacted at more sophisticated levels when no camera was present, the group moderate the evidence they have before them. Eventually the process demands that the group or 'community of practice' (Firth, 2008), identifies a descriptor from the framework which most accurately describes the video as a whole, with over 90 per cent agreement within the group. The out-come cannot find the learner to be sitting across two of the stages, but must determine which one can most safely be agreed on. This 'best fit' approach has been found to be a valuable device to promote analysis and careful consideration about what has been seen and the possible inferences that might be drawn. Agreement is achieved through discussion and voting; when the required majority cannot be achieved, a further video sequence must be identified and discussed.

It is conceded that the choice of footage is a variable element in the process, and that the level of sophistication that the learner achieves can often be linked to the level of experience and interactive skills of their more skilled communicative partner. However, the fact remains that rather than one person reaching a decision about progress which may or may not have occurred over the reporting period, eval-uation in this model is achieved on a piece of incontrovertible evidence with an inter-observer agreement level of over 90 per cent. The group involved in the moderation process has no investment in over estimating their assessment of the evidence, as the process will be repeated at the end of the next cycle so that a continuous record of progress can be achieved.

Avoiding predictive goals

To provide direction and information but avoid prediction, Bayside Special Developmental School in Melbourne, Australia, has recently taken the 'Moderation' process a step further. Using the QCA descrip-tor as the basis of a professional discussion, further consideration takes place to identify what communicative functions and features might have led to a higher-level statement being attributed to the learner. Acknowledging that in many cases, practitioners and learners have developed close social relationships over periods of years of daily contact, a conversation outlining any communicative functions that have been seen to be emerging during their day-to-day interactions takes place. This consideration leads to the construction of a 'learning focus' statement, which makes all practitioners aware of which interactive features and avenues they might usefully draw attention to, or promote opportunities for, within the familiar exploration of their regular interactions. In a discourse which provides the learner with a range of consistently reliable communicative partners and the school with ongoing professional development, the final phase in this process involves staff discussing 'interactive strategies' or how to respond to the learner in a manner which remains familiar and responsive, but might open up opportunities for recognisable variation within the secure context of their interactions. Strategies discussed remain open and completely focused on giving the learner the opportunity to take the lead. They might simply involve using pauses or hesitation at critical points in routine exchanges, varying the vocal intonation of an utterance, or using a lull in an exchange to offer the opportunity to return back to a previously established game 'frame' (Bruner, 1981).

The inherent value of this process is that it reminds both experienced and novice practitioners that there is simply no point in presenting the learner with an opportunity which is too complex for them to interact with successfully, or which is simply mechanistic. Working within the learner's repertoire of understanding ensures that they continue to acquire successful experiences of sustained interaction. Revisiting 'frames' (Bruner, 1981) can be seen to promote contexts for embellishment, elaboration and exploration, whereas single clause exchanges cease to function once the mechanism has been operated.

'For those individuals who consistently fail to show measurable progress on conventional assessments, a different model of progress is required. It is not that these individuals cannot make progress, but (it can be argued) that the instruments by which progress is measured do not suit the people whose abilities are being measured' (Barber and Goldbart, 1998: 114). While the aims and values of the 'producers of outcomes' and the 'meaning makers' clearly differ, the needs of learners with complex and often multiple intellectual disabilities 'to participate in activities which are uniquely human' (Ware, 1994: 13) should remain paramount. Collecting and basing practice on useful evidence is to be encouraged as it promotes reflective discussion and considered intervention strategies. But the need for evidence should not force practitioners to lose sight of the fact that 'there is more to being a member of the human community than the acquisition of minimal independence skills' (Ware, 1994).

☐ Summary

There is a subtle attraction for teachers and therapists to go about the business of promoting communication with people who have profound intellectual disabilities by following the conveniently linear hierarchies that characterise the predominantly assessment-based, commercially available resources.

However by apparently simplifying a learning situation or communicative act by stripping it down to the level of what is observable, the meaning of the actions can be confused and the nature of the activity can easily be lost.

This chapter examined some of the issues which separate the 'performance of communication' from the 'process' of communication and interaction, and questioned the logic of the use of graphics, icons and representations to promote exchanges with learners who are pre-intentional or pre-symbolic. The process of moderating video evidence to report on learning, rather than using predictive goals, was also described.

References

Ainsworth, M.D.S., Blehar, M.C., Waters, E. and Wall, S. (1978) *Patterns of Attachment: A Psychological Study of the Strange Situation.* Hillsdale, NJ: Erlbaum.

Barber, M. (2000) 'Skills, rules, knowledge and Three Mile Island; Accounting for failure to learn among individuals with profound and multiple disabilities', unpublished PhD thesis, Manchester Metropolitan University.

Barber, M. and Goldbart, J. (1998) 'Accounting for learning and failure to learn in people with profound and multiple learning difficulties', in P. Lacey and C. Ouvrey (eds), *People with Profound and Multiple Learning Difficulties: A Collaborative Approach to Meeting Complex Needs.* London: David Fulton.

Barber, M., Goldbart, J. and Munley, G. (1995) 'Student initiations and staff responses: identifying optimal contexts for pupils with profound intellectual disabilities', paper presented to BILD Conference, Oxford, 17 September.

Bates, E., Benigni, L., Bretherton, I., Camaioni, L. and Volterra V. (1979) *The Emergence of Symbols: Cognition and Communication in Infancy.* New York: Academic Press.

Bruner, J.S. (1981) 'Social context of language acquisition', *Language and Communication*, 1: 155–78.

Camaioni, L. (1993) 'The development of intentional communication: a reanalysis', in J. Nadel and L. Camaioni (eds), *New Perspectives in Early Communicative Development*. London: Routledge.

Carter, M. and Iacono, T. (2002) 'Professional judgments of the intentionality of communicative acts', *Augmentative and Alternative Communication*, 18(3): 177–91.

Clegg, J.A., Standen, P.J. and Jones, G. (1996) 'Striking the balance: a grounded theory analysis of staff perspectives', *British Journal of Clinical Psychology*, 35: 249–64.

Collis, M. and Lacey, P. (1996) *Interactive Approaches to Teaching: A Framework for INSET*. London: David Fulton.

Council for Curriculum, Examinations and Assessment (CCEA) (2009) *Quest for Learning; Guidance and Assessment Materials Profound Multiple Learning Difficulties*, National Curriculum Northern Ireland.

Department of Health (DoH) (2009) *Valuing People Now: A New Three-Year Strategy for People with Learning Disabilities*: www.dh.gov.uk/en/Publicationsand-statistics/Publications/PublicationsPolicyandGuidance/DH_093375 (accessed January 2011).

Firth, G. (2008) 'A dual aspect process model of intensive interaction', *British Journal of Learning Disability*, 37: 43–9.

Firth, G. and Barber, M. (2010) *Using Intensive Interaction with a Person with a Social or Communicative Impairment*. London: Jessica Kingsley.

Fogel, A. (1993) *Developing through Relationships: Origins of Communication, Self and Culture*. Chicago, IL: The University of Chicago Press.

Forster, S. and Iacono, T. (2008) 'Disability support workers' experience of interaction with a person with profound intellectual disability', *Journal of Intellectual & Developmental Disability*, 33: 137–47.

Harding, C. (1984) 'Acting with intention: a framework for examining the development of intention to communicate', in L. Feagens, C. Garvey, R. Golinkoff, M.T. Greenberg, C. Harding and J.N. Bohannon (eds), *The Origins and Growth of Communication*. Norwood, NJ: Ablex.

Hewett, D. (2007) 'Do touch: physical contact and people who have severe, profound and multiple learning difficulties', *Support for Learning*, 22(3): 116–23.

Hostyn, I. and Maes, B. (2009) 'Interaction between persons with profound intellectual and multiple disabilities and their partners: a literature review', *Journal of Intellectual and Developmental Disability*, 34(4): 296–312.

Kellett, M. and Nind, M. (2003) *Implementing Intensive Interaction in Schools: Guidelines for Practitioners, Managers and Coordinators*. London: David Fulton.

Light, J. (1988) 'Interaction involving individuals using augmentative and alternative communication systems: state of the art and future directions', *Augmentative and Alternative Communication*, 4: 66–82.

Light, J., Parsons, A. and Drager, K. (2002) 'There's more to life than cookies:

developing interactions for social closeness with beginning communicators who use AAC', in J. Reichle, D.R. Beukelman and J.C. Light (eds), *Exemplary Practices for Beginning Communicators, Implications for AAC*. Baltimore, MD: Brookes.

Nind, M. and Hewett, D. (2001) *A Practical Guide to Intensive Interaction*. Kidderminster: British Institute of Learning Disability.

Olsson, C. (2004) 'Dyadic interaction with a child with multiple disabilities: a system theory perspective on communication', *Augmentative and Alternative Communication*, 20: 228–42.

Qualifications and Curriculum Authority (QCA) (2001) *Planning, Teaching and Assessing the Curriculum for Pupils with Learning Difficulties* (General Guidelines).

Reason, J. (1990) *Human Error*. New York: Cambridge University Press.

Reichle, J., York, J. and Sigafoos, J. (eds) (1991) *Implementing Augmentative and Alternative Communication: Strategies for Learners with Severe Disabilities*. Baltimore: Brookes.

Rice, D. (2009) Personal communication.

Stephenson, J. and Lightfoot, K. (1996) 'Intentional communication and graphic symbol use by students with severe intellectual disability', *International Journal of Disability, Development and Education*, 43(2): 147–65.

Vygotsky, L.S. (1978) *Mind in Society: The Development of Higher Psychological Processes*. Harvard, MA: Harvard University Press.

Ware, J. (1994) 'Using interaction in the education of pupils with PMLDs, (i) creating contingency-sensitive environments', in J. Ware (ed.), *Educating Children with Profound and Multiple Learning Difficulties*. London: David Fulton.

Warren, S. and Yoder, P. (1998) 'Facilitating the transition from preintentional to intentional communication', in A. Wetherby, S. Warren and J. Reichle (eds), *Transition in Prelinguistic Communication*. Baltimore, MD: Paul H. Brookes.

Westwood, R. (2001) *The Language of Organisation*. London: Sage.

7

Intensive Interaction for inclusion and development

Graham Firth

Chapter overview

The establishment of a process of social inclusion through Intensive Interaction is, I believe, the starting point of a developmental process that is well grounded in contemporary learning theory. In this chapter I argue that a combination of research evidence and theoretical models of learning can help build a useful analytic insight into Intensive Interaction practice.

My introduction to Intensive Interaction came when I was teaching adults with severe learning difficulties and/or autism and had spent several years following an 'asocial' curriculum model that excluded any recognition of the students' own motivations and interests. I came to believe that this teaching method failed to address my students' primary learning needs, and also failed to engage the students as adult learners who had their own interests, motivations and means of communication.

With Intensive Interaction I saw the significant possibility of an alternative, socially inclusive curriculum built on developing the learner's current interests and communicative capabilities. Not only did it seem a radical way of conceptualising the teaching/learning process, but it was also in stark contrast to the often fraught imposition of a directive pedagogy and an externally constructed curriculum. With Intensive Interaction I therefore endeavoured to facilitate a more collaborative engagement, built around the notions of 'respect, negotiation and participation' (Nind and Hewett, 1994). Furthermore, there was a change in the power dynamics of the sessions, as the significance of the learning opportunities was now a judgement made by the learner, not by me as the teacher.

A consideration of Intensive Interaction aspects

For many people who have used Intensive Interaction, improved communication and social interaction with clients or students with severe or profound intellectual disabilities is often reported within a surprisingly short time-frame. Although the body of published research is still not extensive (and is open to some methodological criticism) there is a building evidential foundation to support the view that, in the initial stages of meeting people with a severe social or communicative impairment, the use of Intensive Interaction can produce rapid increases in sociable interactivity and thus social inclusion; often in remarkable contrast to previous attempts to engage individuals in more structured or normalised activities.

The initial use of close observation, social availability and lack of demand placed on the person with learning disabilities provides an accessible route to sociable activities. Instances of rapid change in social interactivity are often anecdotally related by practitioners using Intensive Interaction techniques with people for the first time, particularly when employing the techniques of behavioural mirroring or vocal echoing. Additional support for the claims of rapid social inclusion comes from empirical short-term research evidence (for example, Lovell et al., 1998; Zeedyk et al., 2009a, 2009b). Indeed, in the study using micro-analytic analysis of Intensive Interaction by Zeedyk et al. (2009a) it was shown that for all the participants Intensive Interaction was 'effective in promoting social engagement ... well before the end of the first full intervention session', with some changes being seen to 'occur within minutes'.

In addition to the potential for rapid increases in sociable communication over short timescales, experience of using Intensive Interaction over longer periods has demonstrated a 'developmental aspect' as an outcome to systematic and sustained approach adoption. Such extended use of Intensive Interaction has been shown to facilitate gradual development in aspects of communication practice for people with severe or profound intellectual disabilities (Kellett,

2000; Nind, 1996; Watson and Fisher, 1997; Watson and Knight, 1991). Such developmental progression in a person's communicative practice tends to be incremental and thus increases over more extended periods of time, that is, months and years.

Therefore, taken together, the body of Intensive Interaction research demonstrates changes in social responsiveness over differing timescales, and while reflecting on the research evidence and on my own personal experiences of using, and training and supporting others to use Intensive Interaction, I formed the opinion that the measurable outcomes of Intensive Interaction can accrue in two different, but complementary, ways: initially there being a *social inclusion process*, evidenced by an initial rapid expansion of a person's sociability and communicative practice, presumably as latent but previously unacknowledged communicative means are expressed in response to Intensive Interaction techniques. Subsequent to, and dependent on this *social inclusion process*, is a *developmental process* of more incremental communicative skill progression and acquisition. I conceptualised these processes as lying on a continuum, with both process models representing differing temporal aspects of the same phenomenon, that is, a *dual aspect process model* (Figure 7.1) of Intensive Interaction (Firth, 2008).

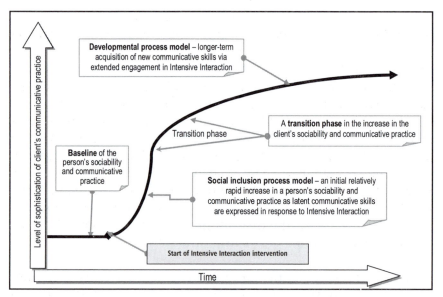

Figure 7.1 A visual representation of the dual aspect process model of Intensive Interaction

Source: Firth (2008)

Lying between these two 'process models' I identified a *transition phase* (similarly described as 'plateauing' in Nind and Hewett, 2005:

134), which is entered as the initial and more rapid expansion of a person's interactive behaviour associated with a social inclusion process subsides and the developmental process begins, with a more incremental development of the learner's sociability and communicative skills.

How learning theory might inform an analysis of Intensive Interaction

Generally, if we wish to analyse any particular issue or activity, and thus develop our understanding, different theoretical models can help us to see things in different ways. More specifically, Intensive Interaction can be viewed from a number of theoretical perspectives, which could lead to different and hopefully useful insights into the approach. We could start with an individualistic analysis focused solely on the actions of, or outcomes for, a single participant in an Intensive Interaction session. Indeed, such analyses are well represented in the current body of literature.

However, as Intensive Interaction is essentially a social process collaboratively undertaken by someone with a social or communicative impairment and a more experienced or expert communication partner, it might also be useful to take a different analytic perspective and look at the interpersonal aspects of Intensive Interaction. For some educational advocates of Intensive Interaction, creating such an interactive partnership is vital in the developmental process of acquiring more sophisticated communication abilities. Such socially supported communicative skill acquisition is well described within the psychological constructivist literature that identifies and describes a process known as 'scaffolding' (Bruner, 1983). Such a process describes the guidance given by a more expert or experienced practitioner that is both supportive and encouraging of the attempts of a novice or less expert practitioner. Indeed, Jerome Bruner (1996) stated that learning or developmental progression is facilitated through 'social transaction rather than solo performance'.

Such a supported developmental or learning process is said to be realised within what Vygotsky (1978) described as the 'zone of proximal development'. This notional cognitive 'zone of proximal development' is hypothesised to lie just in advance of what a person is capable of achieving without support, and straddles the cognitive gap between what a person can do alone and what they can do 'in collaboration with more capable peers' (Vygotsky, 1978: 86). With respect to communication development, such a *social constructivist* view (as proposed by Vygotsky) hypothesises an apprenticeship-like process of supported development, where the learner's development is determined by the social interaction and collaborative activity that is supported and guided by a more expert partner.

It might be useful to look analytically at Intensive Interaction in terms of how it fits with some sociocultural views of learning. Generally, sociocultural views do not take an individualised analytical perspective as far as cognition or knowledge acquisition is concerned. In fact, sociocultural theorists generally show little or no regard for individual aspects of cognition or learning, with learning being seen as 'a process that takes place in a participation framework, not in an individual mind' (Hanks, 1991). Instead they are more concerned with describing human participation in socially organised events. For Intensive Interaction practitioners, sociocultural theorist Barbara Rogoff's 'guided participation' model of learning support (Rogoff, 1990) strikes a resonant chord when describing Intensive Interaction in the initial, exploratory stages. This model of 'guided participation' identifies the collaborative management of roles within an activity to provide the novice practitioner with an appropriate balance between what is reassuringly familiar and what is acceptably challenging (and again this is seen to lie within Vygotsky's 'zone of proximal development').

The sociocultural view frames the mind as socially contextualised rather than individualised, and cognition is seen as an interactional process between an individual and the physical and social environment within which they currently find themselves. According to Lave and Wenger (1991: 53), pioneering theorists in the sociocultural or 'situated' school of learning, 'learning involves the whole person; it implies not only a relation to specific activities, but a relation to social communities'. Learning is seen as 'a process of enculturation into a "community of practice"' (Minick, 1989, in Cobb, 1999: 135), one of the central tenets of the sociocultural view being 'the practical inseparability of individual task performance from social relationships' (Lave and Wenger, 1991: 38).

Another significant aspect of the sociocultural view is the belief in the culturally organised and social nature of knowledge creation. Thus, from this perspective, knowledge is not seen as an individually acquired asset or skill, but instead it is viewed as socially distributed, with social action seen as inseparable from a collaborative process of knowledge creation. As noted above, such a process of collaborative knowledge creation is seen to take place within a socially constructed 'community of practice', with a like-minded group of people building interrelated knowledge and skills through shared experiences, and indeed Lave and Wenger (1991: 98) even suggest that a 'community of practice' is 'an intrinsic condition for the existence of knowledge'. Such a 'community of practice' can be viewed as an informally constructed body of practice based on 'procedural' knowledge and expertise that is developed and subsequently held collectively amongst its constituent members, with novice learners gradually developing their concepts and their practical expertise at a pace that fits their own levels of competence and confidence.

If we are looking to build a description of the process through which social inclusion (for example, via engagement in Intensive Interaction) facilitates developmental progression, sociocultural theories can be useful. They can help us conceptualise how learning concurrently develops from, and is made evident in, the learner's increasing participation in socially organised activity. Lave and Wenger's (1991) sociocultural theory of 'legitimate peripheral participation' can provide a theoretical representation of how a process of authentic engagement in collaborative social activities (for example, Intensive Interaction) is a necessary precursor to social skill acquisition.

With a legitimate peripheral participation (LPP) model (Figure 7.2) there is no linear aspect to skill acquisition, instead we see the development of 'aspects of practice', where skill development is viewed as diffuse and distributed across the particular socially constructed 'community of practice'.

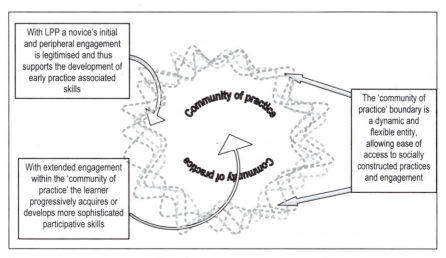

Figure 7.2 Legitimate peripheral participation: learning of practice-associated skills develops through active engagement in a community of practice
Source: Lave and Wenger (1991)

Thus with legitimate peripheral participation, where authentic skill performance and learning are co-dependant, a situation is seen to arise where 'understanding and experience are in constant interaction – indeed, are mutually constitutive' (Lave and Wenger, 1991: 51–2). Such a model can help represent the learning process involved with Intensive Interaction, where a novice interactor, once their emergent communicative and sociable behaviour is acknowledged, legitimised and responded to inclusively, engages in social interactions in gradually more sustained and sophisticated ways, and thus gradually becomes a more central part of an Intensive Interaction 'community of practice', or perhaps more accurately a 'community of intensive interactors'. Initially a person's engagement in such a 'community of intensive interactors' might be halting, tentative and exploratory, however, through repeated joint experience with an experienced interactor, the collaboratively generated social activity is sustained for longer periods of time and develops in sophistication. Thus, through active social inclusion, developmental progress can become manifest as the process of social inclusion continues, and the learner becomes (together with their communication partner) a more skilled practitioner within the 'community of intensive interactors' through increased joint mastery of the necessary skills bounded within this particular community.

However, Intensive Interaction is generally seen to be naturalistic, contingent and even at times intuitive. So it might be useful to ask if a sociocultural view of cognition and learning might offer any useful insights into the practical application of Intensive Interaction. Well, for people with severe or profound intellectual disabilities, or for those with a severe social or communicative impairment, the boundaries of a 'community of intensive interactors' which encompass the skills required to be a member, will need to be made extremely flexible to legitimate any initial and peripheral participation. Such flexibility will then support the learner's initially tentative but active engagement, and their eventual more comprehensive participation. Furthermore, if we are to use such a sociocultural model to inform Intensive Interaction practice, we should perhaps pay more regard to the socially collaborative processes of 'community of practice' generation. Such a 'community of practice' model, more generally, can be seen as informally bringing people who share similar goals and practices together so that they can collaborate with the purpose of achieving their mutually valued goals. Indeed, a 'community of practice' is specifically seen as a group of people 'who share a concern, a set of problems, or a passion about a topic, and who deepen their understanding and knowledge of this area by interacting on an ongoing basis' (Wenger, 1998: 4). This is perhaps a point that needs clearer emphasis – if we accept a 'sociocultural' perspective then there naturally develops a responsibility on the social community around someone to adapt itself to include them, rather than they first having to acquire and pre-emptively evidence the requisite skills to be seen as a 'legitimate' member of an existing social community. As Barber (2000) notes: 'It is not the flexibility of the learner's skills that enables interaction to occur, but the flexibility of the situation that allows the inclusion of the learner.'

From this perspective, if we wish to facilitate learners in joining a 'community of practice' based on Intensive Interaction principles and techniques, the learner will require easy and peripheral access to the social activities included in the 'community of intensive interactors'. However, with the traditional interpretation of legitimate peripheral participation such 'communities of practice' (CoP) are already in existence for newcomers to join and become accepted members within. This is not generally the case for learners with severe or profound intellectual disabilities, or those who are socially isolated. For such learners positive action will be required to create such 'communities' with the sole purpose of the learner's eventual active participation. From this perspective, the initial participation of the learner will require some kind of 'community of practice' to be actively created that allows them frequent access to the kinds of activities included in any 'community of intensive interactors'. This will therefore require the adoption by staff or carers of behaviours and responses uniquely attuned to the learner's current behavioural repertoire, their personal motivating factors, and their communicative or potential communicative strengths. Subsequently, the cooperatively developed actions of Intensive Interaction can then become gradually extended through the simultaneous building of both the repertoire of activities and the underpinning social relationship. As this process continues, both parties can then become more centrally functioning members of an inclusive and responsive 'community of intensive interactors'.

This 'CoP' model could also usefully be employed as an analytic framework with which to explore the learning processes of a number of students (or clients) with whom Intensive Interaction is used in an educative manner – that being particularly useful within an identifiable collective or 'class' setting. The creation of an informal but dynamic and supportive communication learning environment, one that allows for easy access to authentic communication activities, will more likely parallel the early communication experiences created naturally within the 'infant–caregiver' dyad or social family environment. Thus it could certainly be argued that the deliberate creation of a 'CoP' classroom, one that is actively made abundant in genuine and affirming communication experiences, will more effectively promote the successful learning of fundamental communication practices.

However, this is perhaps a significant challenge to the educational or developmental use of Intensive Interaction, as we are intentionally facilitating the development of aspects of social practice that cannot be individually expressed (or assessed) outside of an interactive environment. Indeed, it would seem, from this analytical perspective we are perhaps creating greater social interdependence for our learners, and not creating individualised skills and knowledge (the usual objective of most educational interventions). This interdependence, however, mirrors real life social scenarios and relationship building, in that we are all mutually dependent on each other to support our own social interactivity via our shared cultural understanding and interests. Equally, with the support of staff or carers using Intensive Interaction, we should be actively creating the same social context for our clients or learners.

Some discussion on the nature of knowledge with respect to Intensive Interaction

As well as undertaking an analysis of the learning processes involved in Intensive Interaction, a similar analysis might be useful when looking to understand the nature of any actual learning thus created. However, there are a number of competing views or interpretations as to the actual nature of any learning or knowledge that accrues or is constructed from engaging in different types of learning activities.

Initially, and perhaps simplistically, if we were to analyse the engagement of a person with learning disabilities in the process of Intensive Interaction, this might lead us to view their learning in terms of them developing, or 'constructing', an individual understanding of the nature and uses of fundamental communication and sociability practices (for example, the communicative nature and uses of eye contact, physical contact, vocalisations, joint behavioural sequencing and/or turn-taking). Of course, not all the learning takes place on the part of the learning disabled person, and it could be argued that during the early 'social inclusion' process of Intensive Interaction, any learning that does accrue will most likely be that developed by the practitioner or communication partner. Thus practical engagement in the process of Intensive Interaction will facilitate the development of 'procedural knowledge' (that is, knowledge of procedures and/or practical actions) on the part of the practitioner about what a person with a communicative or social impairment can and will actually do in terms of their communication practice.

More generally, proponents of differing theoretical perspectives hold differing views as to the nature of any knowledge that results from a given learning experience. According to one theoretician, Sfard (1998) there are two distinct metaphorical categorisations or conceptualisations that can be applied to knowledge itself, and although she argued that discreet metaphorical categorisations can be problematic, the use of such conceptual metaphors can help us reflect on the processes underlying different learning scenarios.

First, Sfard identifies an *acquisition metaphor* for knowledge, and this is applicable in circumstances when a learner is seen to be individually accumulating or even passively absorbing discrete and unproblematic knowledge in such a way that it can be applied to, or recalled and used individualistically within a given situation. When conceptualising learning in such metaphorical terms, any knowledge is seen as abstracted from any process of task performance, and therefore is viewed as a decontextualised cognitive representation or structure. Such knowledge is sometimes termed *declarative, conceptual* and/or *theoretical* knowledge, and is the type that can be recalled, expressed and shared, mainly through symbolic means.

In contrast, Sfard's *participation metaphor* replaces the idea of acquired decontextualised knowledge with a more adaptive conceptualisation of learning, where 'knowing' replaces the idea of 'having knowledge' and participation in activities is seen as analytically more relevant than the acquisition and storage of knowledge through individualised cognitive structures. When using such a participation metaphor as an analytic tool, instead of an experience being seen to generate decontextualised knowledge, this view is replaced by the concept of contextualised or 'situated' knowing, with such knowing being seen as 'inseparable from the occasions and activities of which it is the product' (Bredo, 1999: 35). As such this knowing could be viewed as synonymous with the 'aspects of practice' associated with the 'community of practice' model, such knowing being postulated as being created through collaborative participation in authentic activity where 'things gain meaning by being used in a shared experience or joint action' (Dewey, 1916, cited in Bredo, 1999: 19). Such knowledge, or knowing, is therefore viewed as socially diffuse in nature, that is, it is distributed socially or held collectively by the participants in the given activity. Indeed, the social context for knowledge application and expression is seen as inseparable from the collaborative process of knowledge creation, with both processes contemporaneously occurring within a given 'community of practice', where 'knowledge guides action, and action guides knowledge' (McCormick, 1999: 126).

Using the more dynamic descriptive term of 'knowing' where knowledge can be seen as more 'situated' or even tacit within an activity, such knowledge can in reality only be revealed or expressed when a person is actually engaged in that activity. Such tacit 'knowing' is often not available to us to symbolically express or reflect on outside of the context of the activity to which it is related. Furthermore, from this sociocultural or 'situated' perspective, it is the level of active participation in any activity that is seen as analytically significant, rather than an individual's possession of, and ability to recall decontextualised knowledge. Interestingly, there are many anecdotal observations that some people just 'do' Intensive Interaction, without any formal training or even having heard of the approach. Presumably this is because they have the required tacit 'knowing' that enables them to respond at some intuitive level to the person, possibly by employing previously developed and currently tacit caregiver interactional knowledge (Nind and Thomas, 2005).

As far as Intensive Interaction is concerned, instead of the participants accumulating decontextualised individual 'knowledge', the collaboratively constructed interactional process allows for the development of skills or specific 'aspects of practice' related to social interaction or fundamental communication, thus illustrating the 'context specific nature of knowledge' (McCormick, 1999: 127). At the same time any such development will then become observable in the progressive increase in the sociable practices of the participants.

Another issue seen as significant from the sociocultural viewpoint is the interconnectedness of knowledge construction and notions of individual identity or esteem, and according to Greeno et al. (1999: 139) there is 'a duality between membership in a community and issues of self-perception and identity'. Barbara Rogoff, a leading proponent of the sociocultural view, highlighted 'identity' as highly significant when proposing that 'the formation of a sense of identity is learning, and the identity itself is knowledge' (The Open University, E836 Study Guide: 125). Thus a person's view of themselves, or their sense of their own agency and esteem, should never be too far from our minds when we engage in potential learning activities, and perhaps this is especially so if the potential learner has severe or profound intellectual disabilities and/or autism.

From the Intensive Interaction practitioner's point of view, a change in identity for a learner from someone who is a socially passive individual, to someone who sees themselves as both socially significant and an active participant in increasingly sophisticated and temporally extended social interactions may be the most significant learning outcome. Thus Intensive Interaction can empower people as active participants in the process of learning about themselves and others as social beings, promoting their sense of esteem and social agency, which according to Bruner (1999: 174) 'are central to the construction of a concept of self'.

Some implications coming from the analytic process

Following from the previous sections of this chapter, it appears that some analysis using accepted theoretical models of learning might be useful in terms of legitimising the current practice of Intensive Interaction practitioners across a number of disciplines. With respect to the *dual aspect process model of Intensive Interaction* (Firth, 2008), for certain individual practitioners or professional groups, one process model rather than the other might more naturally fit with their individual philosophy, or their particular aims when using the approach. For example, a shorter term *social inclusion process model* might be more appropriate for residential care staff or day centre staff, while a *developmental process model* should fit more naturally with the learning aims of educational staff. I also believe that greater clarity in articulating the primary aims of an Intensive Interaction intervention is beneficial, so that those being trained or supported in using the approach might be better able to conceptualise what is expected of them, and thus better able to make judgements on the effectiveness of the approach and on their own Intensive Interaction practice.

In terms of actual practice, if practitioners have different aims for the approach, there may also be associated differences in how Intensive Interaction is procedurally employed. It could be that a social inclusion process would lead to a more integrated or opportunistic application of the approach, while a developmental process might lead to a more pre-planned, focused and sessional intervention. The issues of record-keeping and evidence gathering might also be addressed differently, with one process model requiring the collection of data evidencing instances of social inclusion, and the other process model requiring objectified evidence of developmental progression, especially at or after the transition phase when any easily discernable gains will have begun to plateau.

Looking again at the 'community of practice' model previously noted, as Lave and Wenger point out, 'learning must be understood with respect to a practice as a whole, with its multiplicity of relations – both within the community [of practice] and with the world at large' (1991: 114). This important point illustrates the potential that the sociable activities employed during Intensive Interaction may not be authentic to a person's general social situation outside of any Intensive Interaction session. Thus any knowledge and skills that are collaboratively constructed via Intensive Interaction can only be expressed with the active participation of other members of a 'community of intensive interactors', that is, other Intensive Interaction practitioners. It is therefore vitally important that all staff or carers need to know how to apply Intensive Interaction with the people that they care for or work with, otherwise any communicative and social development made by a person will not generalise across to other social situations.

Therefore one potential development of this analytic process is that instead of viewing an Intensive Interaction practitioner's role being simply as a communication partner or developmental facilitator, they should also acknowledge some responsibility for the creation of a wider 'community of intensive interactors'. Such an interactive 'community' would then be more universally available to all potential learners with severe or profound intellectual disabilities. The ultimate aspiration should not just be limited to developing successful interactions with someone with severe or profound intellectual disabilities within a set location and during a set time, but instead to enable meaningful and developmentally beneficial interactions to be engaged in by a person at any time or place that is appropriate. This will therefore require a wider dissemination of the rationale, philosophy and procedural aspects of Intensive Interaction, so that eventually an increasing number of people who regularly have contact with a person with a social or communicative impairment will be able to engage them with individually appropriate Intensive Interaction practices.

Another challenge highlighted by the analytical tools of legitimate peripheral participation and Sfard's metaphors of knowledge, is that any assessment of developmental progression can only be judged on the collaborative level of 'participation', and not on any individualised expression of previously 'acquired' skills and knowledge. The usual ostensibly objectivised methods of individual assessment cannot be employed to measure a person's level of engagement in a 'community of practice'. Only a system that can differentiate between, and thus evidence, increasing levels of social engagement, from the earliest levels of peripheral participation through to more central and sustained involvement should be considered for such a purpose.

An example of such a system is the 'Framework for Recognising Attainment'[1] (QCDA, 2009), which was specifically designed to be used across the curriculum for students with severe or profound intellectual disabilities. This framework employs a series of graded definitions indicating the level of engagement of any participant, during any activity or interactive episode. These definitions, further developed for use with Intensive Interaction (Firth, 2010), are:

> **Encounter:** the student or client is present during an interactive episode without any obvious awareness of its progression, *for example, a willingness to tolerate a shared social atmosphere or environment is sufficient.*

> **Awareness:** the student or client appears to notice, or fleetingly focus on an event or person involved in the interactive episode, *for example, by briefly interrupting a pattern of self-absorbed movement or vocalisation.*

> **Attention and response:** the student or client begins to respond (although not consistently) to what is happening in an interactive episode, *for example, by showing signs of surprise, enjoyment, frustration or dissatisfaction.*

> **Engagement:** the student or client shows consistent attention to the interactive episode presented to them, *for example, by sustained looking or listening, or repeatedly following events with movements of their eyes, head or other body parts.*

> **Participation:** the student or client shows anticipation of, and engages in, taking turns in a sequence of events during an interactive episode, *for example, by intentionally sequencing their actions with another person or by intentionally passing signals repeatedly back and forth.*

> **Involvement:** the student or client makes active efforts to reach out, consistently join in, or even comment in some way on the interaction, *for example, by sequencing their actions and speaking, signing, vocalising or gesturing in some consistent and meaningful way.*

Also, coming from the 'community of practice' model of analysis, extended engagement in such a community is seen as a prerequisite of knowledge creation and conceptual development. Thus, to generate continued and sustained community membership any Intensive

Interaction training schedule should not be planned as a short-term intervention or a single training experience. Sustainability will need to be planned for within an extended training package to keep members involved in constructing and supporting the development of a 'community of intensive interactors'. Such sustained staff or carer engagement will need to provide practitioners with continued access to further knowledge or experiences that will help to refine and enrich their understanding of Intensive Interaction theory and practice. This is no meagre ambition, as it will require sustained and significant support due to the high level of resources required. However, with the inclusion of Intensive Interaction in the UK policy document *Valuing People Now* (DoH, 2009) there is a growing expectation that such an ambition should be met.

☐ Summary

This chapter is designed to help Intensive Interaction practitioners analyse and identify their main purposes in employing the approach. It is also intended to provide a clear rationale for the sustainable development of Intensive Interaction, one that will involve more systemic changes, so that the approach will no longer be viewed as an elective intervention. As noted above, in the recent UK government publication *Valuing People Now: A New Three-Year Strategy for People with Learning Disabilities* (DoH, 2009) an explicit policy aim is that, when addressing the needs of people with profound intellectual disabilities, delivering a high-quality and personalised service is dependent upon 'recognising that the very particular support needs of an individual will mean very individualised support packages, including systems for facilitating meaningful two-way communication' (DoH, 2009: 37).

For many people with severe or profound intellectual disabilities, 'facilitating meaningful two-way communication' can only truly come about by the adequately resourced, systematic and sustainable use of Intensive Interaction.

Note

1 The framework is based on the work of Aitken and Buultjens (1992), Brown (1996) and McInness and Treffry (1982).

References

Aitken, S. and Buultjens, M. (1992) *Vision for Doing*. Edinburgh: Moray House School of Education.

Barber, M. (2000) 'The teacher who mistook his pupil for a nuclear incident: environmental influences on the learning of people with profound and multiple learning disabilities: http://drmarkbarber.co.uk/Publications.htm#actual (accessed 8 May 2007).

Bredo, E. (1999) 'Reconstructing educational psychology', in P. Murphy (ed.), *Learners, Learning & Assessment*. London: Paul Chapman Publishing.

Brown, E. (1996) *Religious Education for All*. London: David Fulton Publishers.

Bruner, J. (1983) *Child's Talk: Learning to Use Language*. New York: Oxford University Press.

Bruner, J. (1996) *The Culture of Education*. Cambridge, MA: Harvard University Press.

Bruner, J. (1999) 'Culture, mind and education', in B. Moon and P. Murphy (eds), *Curriculum in Context*. London: Paul Chapman Publishing.

Department of Health (DoH) (2009) *Valuing People Now: A New Three-Year Strategy for People with Learning Disabilities*: www.dh.gov.uk/en/Publications andstatistics/Publications/PublicationsPolicyandGuidance/DH_093375 (accessed 15 January 2010).

Dewey, J. (1916) *Democracy* and *Education*. New York: Macmillan.

Firth, G. (2008) 'A dual aspect process model of Intensive Interaction', *British Journal of Learning Disabilities*, 37: 43–9.

Firth, G. (2010) *A Framework for Recognising Attainment in Intensive Interaction*. Leeds: Leeds Partnerships NHS Trust.

Greeno, J., Pearson, P. and Schoenfeld, A. (1999) 'Achievement and theories of knowing and learning', in R. McCormick and C. Paechter (eds), *Learning & Knowledge*. London: Paul Chapman Publishing.

Hanks, W. (1991) 'Foreword', in J. Lave and E. Wenger (eds), *Situated Learning: Legitimate Peripheral Participation*. New York: Cambridge University Press.

Kellett, M. (2000) 'Sam's story: evaluating intensive interaction in terms of its effect on the social and communicative ability of a young child with severe learning difficulties', *Support for Learning*, 15(4): 165–71.

Lave, J. and Wenger, E. (1991) *Situated Learning: Legitimate Peripheral Participation*. New York: Cambridge University Press.

Lovell, D., Jones, R. and Ephraim, G. (1998) 'The effect of Intensive Interaction on the sociability of a man with severe intellectual disabilities', *International Journal of Practical Approaches to Disability*, 22(2/3): 3–8.

McCormick, R. (1999) 'Practical knowledge: a view from the snooker table', in R. McCormick and C. Paechter (eds), *Learning & Knowledge*. London: Paul Chapman Publishing.

McInness, J. and Treffry, J. (1982) *Deaf-blind Infants and Children: A Developmental Guide*. Toronto: University of Toronto Press.

Minick, N.J. (1989) 'L. S. Vygotsky and Soviet activity theory: new perspectives on the relationship between learners and society', in P. Cobb (1989) 'Where is the mind?', in P. Murphy (ed.), *Learners, Learning and Assessment*. London: Open University Press.

Nind, M. (1996) 'Efficacy of Intensive Interaction: developing sociability and communication in people with severe and complex learning difficulties using an approach based on caregiver–infant interaction', *European Journal of Special Educational Needs*, 11(1): 48–66.

Nind, M. and Hewett, D. (1994) *Access to Communication: Developing the Basics of Communication with People with Severe Learning Difficulties through Intensive Interaction.* London: David Fulton.

Nind, M. and Hewett, D. (2005) *Access to Communication: Developing the Basics of Communication with People with Severe Learning Difficulties through Intensive Interaction*, 2nd edn. London: David Fulton.

Nind, M. and Thomas, G. (2005) 'Reinstating the value of teachers' tacit knowledge for the benefit of learners: using "Intensive Interaction"', *Journal of Research in Special Educational Needs*, 5(3): 97–100.

The Open University (1999) *E836: Learning, Curriculm and Assessment.* Milton Keynes: The Open University.

Qualification and Curriculum Development Agency (QCDA) (2009) *Planning, Teaching and Assessing the Curriculum for Pupils with Learning Difficulties*: www.qcda.gov.uk/resources/assets/P_scales_Guidelines.pdf (accessed January 2011).

Rogoff, B. (1990) *Apprenticeships in Thinking: Cognitive Development in Social Context.* New York: Oxford University Press.

Sfard, A. (1998) 'On two *metaphors* for learning and the dangers of choosing just one', *Educational Researcher,* 27(2): 4–13.

Vygotsky, L.S. (1978) *Mind and Society: The Development of Higher Mental Processes.* Cambridge, MA: Harvard University Press.

Watson, J. and Fisher, A. (1997) 'Evaluating the effectiveness of Intensive Interaction teaching with pupils with profound and complex learning disabilities', *The British Journal of Special Education*, 24(2): 80–7.

Watson, J. and Knight, C. (1991) 'An evaluation of Intensive Interactive teaching with pupils with very severe learning difficulties', *Child Language Teaching and Therapy*, 7(3): 310–25.

Wenger, E. (1998) *Communities of Practice: Learning, Meaning, and Identity.* Cambridge: Cambridge University Press.

Zeedyk, S., Caldwell, P. and Davies, C. (2009a) 'How rapidly does Intensive Interaction promote social engagement for adults with profound learning disabilities and communicative impairments?', *European Journal of Special Needs Education*, 24(2): 119–37.

Zeedyk, S., Davies, C., Parry, S. and Caldwell, P. (2009b) 'Fostering social engagement in Romanian children with communicative impairments', *British Journal of Learning Disabilities*, 37(3): 186–96.

8

Intensive Interaction within models of organisational change

Cath Irvine

Chapter overview

This chapter discusses the dissemination process of Intensive Interaction so far. Of particular interest is why Intensive Interaction has taken so long to become accepted and more widely used. Although I frequently use the term 'dissemination', I make reference to the terminology discussed by Greenhalgh et al. (2004: 582) who describe dissemination as 'active and planned efforts to persuade target groups to adopt an innovation' and 'diffusion' which is described as a 'passive spread'. The chapter also briefly examines some processes around innovation and organisational change in relation to the past, present and future propagation and support of Intensive Interaction. The discussions are illustrated throughout the chapter with examples from my own work, as well as observations and/or discussions with Intensive Interaction colleagues.

When I first discovered Intensive Interaction and began to implement it in my clinical role as a speech and language therapist in adult learning disability services, I knew very little about the processes of innovation, dissemination or organisational change. I was to face a steep learning curve! Along with an ever-increasing number of other people I was directly involved in the changes that were necessary, from first introducing the approach into my work place, to having it very nearly fully embedded into services for adults with learning disabilities across the county. This took nine years (Irvine, 1998). Few of the people involved in this innovation knew the relevant theories for what we were undertaking. We did what appeared to be sensible and necessary within our own situation.

Within services for people with learning disabilities, hundreds of Intensive Interaction practitioners have undertaken the role of introducing Intensive Interaction to their work place or family. Many, like me, will have discovered that the introduction of new approaches is a long, hard slog, as Rosenfeld and Servo (1990: 29) would concur: 'Innovation almost always involves a prolonged battle amongst numerous people and requires tremendous stamina and confidence on the part of a champion.'

Since 2005, my work has consisted of introducing or re-invigorating Intensive Interaction practice within different organisations, and seeking best practice for having systemic and sustainable use of the approach within each setting. Intensive Interaction has been around for over 20 years and yet it is still possible to come across services for people with severe/profound learning disabilities and/or autism who have never heard of it, have heard of it but never tried it, have tried it but did not keep it going or have used it for gaining access to a withdrawn person but have not experienced long-term implementation to aid development of new skills.

The challenges of Intensive Interaction propagation

With the advantage of hindsight, the early propagation of Intensive Interaction involved some specific issues that created potential barriers to any prospective practitioners. It seems to me that among these was that, first, Intensive Interaction appeared to contradict service approaches of the era and required philosophical and cultural changes in organisations. Secondly, Intensive Interaction was at first given away freely and openly with no support mechanisms or restrictions on use for practitioners. Finally, the dissemination needed to be across differing professions, organisations and target age groups.

The philosophical and cultural contradictions

My memories of services for people with learning disabilities and autism in the late 1980s and early 1990s were that they were largely dominated by behavioural methods of working which were so well entrenched that Intensive Interaction most probably appeared to be anathema in the free-flowing, seemingly unstructured and equality based foundations (Nind and Hewett, 1994). Alongside this, the frequently misunderstood principles of normalisation meant that sitting with a person on their level, playing and probably sharing some elements of physical contact was to defy accepted service approaches of the era. The introduction and continuation of the National Curriculum in education probably created further confusion for people wishing to establish Intensive Interaction in schools. See Dave Hewett's observations elsewhere in this volume.

When the staff group at Harperbury Hospital School in Hertfordshire began the gruelling but invigorating process of developing and researching the reflective and evaluative system that is Intensive Interaction, their barriers to innovation and the ensuing dissemination within their own school were reduced by having a wealth of positive factors in place. Most of the team were enthused by the new approach, participating in the developments and sharing ownership. There was total support from the middle management, in fact, they shared in or were driving the participation. Within this atmosphere, the challenges of behaviourism and normalisation could be discussed and re-evaluated in the light of the efficacy of Intensive Interaction (see Nind and Hewett, 2005).

The wider challenge that Intensive Interaction innovation presented emerged once the tweaking, adjusting and celebrating were completed at Harperbury, and people in other organisations began to show an interest in using the approach. While the originators were keen to share their innovation with others, every organisation that heard about Intensive Interaction was responsible for their own dissemination and as Rosenfeld and Servo (1990: 31) propose:

> Common places for an idea to be dropped within complex organisations are with:
> * the idea originator
> * middle management
> * across organisational boundaries.

Thus, as the work of the Harperbury team began to reach out, many services that were interested in Intensive Interaction had to begin re-evaluating many of the, I believe, deeply entrenched attitudes that were common in working with people with learning disabilities. I have worked with or spoken to many brave practitioners who attempted to introduce Intensive Interaction to their services. They chronicle the difficulties of keeping themselves enthused and convincing middle managers of the efficacy of Intensive Interaction. There was also the gradual realisation of the need to negotiate the cultural change that would be necessary for implementation, and find the confidence to use Intensive Interaction themselves in settings where the required behaviour was often seen as unacceptable or strange. Each of these practitioners became innovators in their own right.

People who heard about Intensive Interaction in the early days did so through conferences and journal articles in the late eighties and, in 1994, the publication of *Access to Communication* (Nind and Hewett, 1994). There was also the slow ripple effect of the many one-day introduction courses commenced by Nind and Hewett in the late 1980s and carried through to this day, which contribute to the continuing diffusion and dissemination of the approach.

My perception is that for the last 20 years it has been chiefly Intensive Interaction practitioners rather than managers who have pioneered the introduction of the approach into services. Most probably, these practitioners had little strategic influence over organisational or cultural change and where change has occurred, it has often been slow, diffusive and punctuated with false starts.

Conversely, although difficult to evidence, I wonder how learning disability services would have developed had Intensive Interaction not been regularly discussed for 20 years. Perhaps behavioural approaches would have continued to dominate the lives of people with learning disabilities and/or autism. My belief is that a very slow, diffusive and participative change (see the 'Organisational issues' section below) has happened across services just because Intensive Interaction was there in the consciousness, even when not being constructively implemented.

In projects where I have been involved in introducing Intensive Interaction to services, one of the by-products of the dissemination has been that services have had to re-examine their policies, practices and thinking around influential issues such as age appropriateness and physical contact. It is my belief that the use of Intensive Interaction has been responsible in changing service cultures towards a more person-centred way of thinking.

In the current era of person-centred thinking and the references to Intensive Interaction in *Valuing People Now* (DoH, 2009) and within the national curriculum guidelines for learning difficulties, many barriers to the use of Intensive Interaction have diminished; however, some do remain. The tasklessness and lack of predetermined targets in Intensive Interaction continue to challenge the way in which services are organised. The task for the wider Intensive Interaction community in overcoming these hurdles is to determinedly and consistently educate advisers, inspection bodies, head teachers and managers about the efficacy of the approach through regular hands-on practice, evaluation and research.

Free and open dissemination

Intensive Interaction was first made public at a conference in 1987 (see Hewett and Nind, 1988) and followed up by an article in the *British Journal of Special Education* in 1988 (Nind and Hewett, 1988). From that point on, Intensive Interaction was introduced into some services, and journal articles and informal papers written about early implementation credit Melanie Nind and Dave Hewett for their support (see Knight and Watson, 1990).

In education at the time in many places there was a greater culture than now of action research and free sharing of good practice (for example, see Somekh et al., 1987). The early propagation of Intensive Interaction reflects Nind and Hewett's association with this culture. It was in this spirit that Intensive Interaction was available, at no cost and with no restrictions, to whoever had the motivation to introduce it to their work place.

However, there were a number of potential problems in that people trying the approach had no definite reassurance that they were doing it correctly and this insecurity may have affected the enthusiasm that is necessary in any new innovation.

While Intensive Interaction is an approach that is free-flowing, relaxed and makes use of natural, spontaneous behaviours, there is an implicit standard of practice in that it reflects the best of parent/carer interactions with a young infant. However Intensive Interaction has, at times, been misrepresented into what Melanie Nind calls 'hybrids' or 'weak imitations' (Nind, 2006). I have come across people who have interpreted Intensive Interaction as cold imitation, entertaining, stimulating, talking at, or insisting on being given attention from the learner, rather than the waiting, watching, interacting, responding and talking with that is implicit in the approach that was developed at Harperbury.

More recently, strategies have been introduced to aid true dissemination: 'active and planned efforts to persuade target groups to adopt an innovation' (Greenhalgh et al., 2004: 582). Accredited Intensive Interaction coordinators courses and the Assessed Practitioner course provide individuals and organisations options for achieving recognised good practice. Intensive Interaction regional support groups offer support to individual practitioners. Recent publications putting even further emphasis on the detail of good Intensive Interaction technique (Firth and Barber, 2010) and the posting of documents such as 'What Intensive Interaction is and what Intensive Interaction isn't' on the Intensive Interaction website also help to clarify some of the differences between the approach developed at Harperbury and some of the hybrids that may have emerged over time.

Dissemination across differing professions and organisations

Intensive Interaction crosses boundaries at the highest of levels, involving the ministerial departments of health, social care and education. It crosses boundaries of services for different age groups, from early years to elderly. It crosses boundaries with target client groups, and is being used with people with learning disabilities and autism (Nind and Hewett, 1994, 2005), social deprivation (Zeedyk et al., 2009), dementia (Ellis and Astell, 2008) and, though as yet unpublished, I am aware of a number of practitioners using Intensive Interaction with people with acquired brain injuries. As can be seen from the literature, Intensive Interaction crosses boundaries of professions: the originators, Nind and Hewett and the staff at Harperbury School were from education, as were Kellett (Kellett, 2004), Barber (Barber, 2007, 2008) and Firth (Firth, 2008); Samuel (Samuel, 2001) and Elgie and McGuire (Elgie and McGuire, 2001) are psychologists; Irvine (Irvine, 2001) and Crabbe (Crabbe, 2007) represent speech and language therapy.

In my thinking and planning around Intensive Interaction implementation I find myself not only introducing the approach to hands-on practitioners, but also targeting three areas of extended practitioner and Intensive Interaction support. In my experience, addressing these wider issues increases the sustainable use of the approach. They are as follows:

- organisational
- professional
- national strategic.

I give an example of these divisions with a brief account of my own early work in introducing Intensive Interaction to the work place.

In my early years as a specialist speech and language therapist for people with learning disabilities, I overheard part of a conversation that went: 'We don't do signing in art with Simon because he has a communication group on Wednesdays.' This snippet of insight resulted in me disbanding all communication groups and investing my time in embedding total communication practices into the daily life, sessions and activities of the day centre and homes in the geographical area in which I was working. Thus, I was prepared when introducing Intensive Interaction to ensure that the responsibility for daily use was quickly transferred to direct care and development staff and their management. I was extremely fortunate in that the staff in Social Services had been agitating for more effective strategies for working with people with profound and multiple learning disabilities, so were receptive to the introduction of Intensive Interaction. Management of Social Services were quickly convinced of the efficacy, and were supportive after seeing individuals' lives improve. Due to these circumstances, my motivation remained high.

The dilemmas persisted though: having introduced Intensive Interaction first to day services, residential services were slow to respond to invitations to get involved in the approach (organisational issue); psychology had been supportive during the initial research project (Irvine, 1998) but found it difficult to commit time to long-term involvement (professional issue); Intensive Interaction was introduced in one of the four geographical areas of the county for which I had clinical responsibility, and the other three areas were clamouring for similar input (organisational issue).

Nine years later we had largely overcome these challenges and had very thoroughly moved the ownership and responsibility of Intensive Interaction from speech and language therapy to the services who were working directly and on a day-to-day basis with the people for whom Intensive Interaction was relevant. However, we had so far had little effect on private care services, early years services and education (national strategic issue). I take each of these issues in turn.

Organisational issues

It is my impression that many innovations struggle in similar ways to Intensive Interaction in crossing even some of the smallest organisational barriers. For example, I regularly speak to teachers who have a strong culture of signing and/or Intensive Interaction in their class-room, but worry about the children they have been teaching moving into new classes where these approaches will not be sustained.

I have had discussions with residential staff who do not see Intensive Interaction and/or signing as their job, but something that will be done at day centres or during therapy, rather than as a holistic approach to communication, learning, quality of life, person-centredness and respect. Conversely I have had discussions with frustrated residential staff who use Intensive Interaction and/or signing, but cannot persuade the day provision staff to participate.

One gentleman who was receiving Intensive Interaction at a day centre built up a repertoire which included turn-taking in banging his hands on the arms of his chair and laughing together with staff when they mirrored this behaviour. However, in his residential home (run by the same organisation) the staff discouraged him from banging his chair and he would be reprimanded whenever he did so. It appeared that he, as a gentleman with profound dis-abilities, was expected to learn when it was appropriate to display invitations to interact rather than the residential staff learning to participate in an approach through which he was making good progress.

The examples above illustrate organisations that have not yet devel-oped an overall culture of shared practice, shared values and working intentions, sometimes even within rooms next door to one another in the same work place. We probably all know of many similar exam-ples of a mismatch between family members, schools, residential establishments and day provisions for adults.

Managers within organisations bear some responsibility for the pro-vision of shared practices, values and working intentions. Managers are often inundated with a variety of innovations promoted by a variety of sources ranging from governmental, local authorities, cli-nicians and their own staff. If innovations and new approaches are to be sustainable then managers need to constantly and consistently weigh the efficacies of new innovations and retain a clear focus on how these innovations reflect their value base.

As Kotter and Hesketh (2008: 65) argue, a shared value base can be instrumental in accepting new approaches no matter who initiates them: 'When these initiatives come from middle or lower levels in the firm, they are usually supported by more senior managers because they share the values that motivated the initiatives in the first place.'

With the organisational issues outlined above in mind, my work to embed Intensive Interaction within organisations includes, along with the support of hands-on practitioners, the forming of a multi-agency, multidisciplinary strategy group to support, advocate and resource Intensive Interaction practitioners.

This group helps the dissemination, education and acceptance process across the organisation and frees practitioners to concentrate on their day-to-day use of Intensive Interaction knowing that potential blockages will be dealt with at a strategic level. The necessity for forming such a group is best underpinned by the theories of 'participative' and 'directive change'. While the original source is unknown, Figure 8.1 was first published by Hersey and Blanchard (1972) to support their discussions around participative and directive change, and is still useful in understanding and applying the theory to the dissemination of Intensive Interaction.

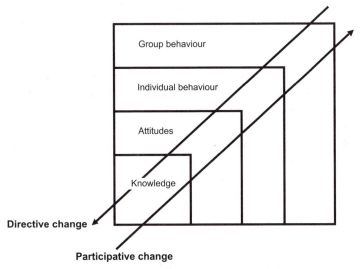

Group behaviour

Individual behaviour

Attitudes

Knowledge

Directive change

Participative change

Figure 8.1 Differing directions of organisation change
Source: Hersey and Blanchard (1972)

As the name suggests, participative change is a change that operates from the coalface of organisations, and in the Intensive Interaction context this means individual practitioners who have introduced the approach to the work place. Participative change can be diffusive, slow and evolutionary but lasts longer because people generally come to believe in what they are doing. Participative change is intrinsic, rather than extrinsically and externally driven. Members of staff have time to adjust gradually, and resistance is low.

Hersey and Blanchard (1972) propose that participative change begins with extending people's knowledge – which in Intensive Interaction terms would mean ensuring people are aware of the practice, the underlying theories and the evidence from research. This knowledge would then challenge attitudes, particularly around the nature of, for instance, play, equality and respect of the individual. Good quality training can provide a safe space for these transitions in knowledge and attitudes to take place relatively rapidly. Knowledge and attitudinal change would result in a change of the individual's behaviour in that they would begin to use Intensive Interaction themselves. As the process of change is extended to other people, group behaviour is altered, managers support the innovation, and dissemination occurs to the point that Intensive Interaction becomes the cultural norm and those people who will not use the approach stand out against the critical mass of those who do participate.

This naturally explains the slow spread of Intensive Interaction. The aspiration from the beginning that Intensive Interaction would be shared by participative change (even though the originators would probably not have described it like that) ensured this sense of 'slow burn' right across services nationwide.

Classically, unless managers are operating with the positive optimum style envisioned by Kotter and Hesketh (2008), participative change could be frustrated by managers and/or clinicians who are not supportive of the use of the innovation. The creation of a multidisciplinary, multi-agency strategy group at an early stage addresses this potential block in support and begins the dissemination within the organisation.

Alternatively, directive change is imposed by managers in the assumption that the group will respond by changing their behaviours as ordered. It can create resistance and short-term changes in behaviour which are often only demonstrated in the presence of a manager. The change is extrinsic rather than intrinsic as Greenhalgh et al. (2004: 599–600) point out: 'Authoritarian decisions often increase initial adoption (people have no choice) but reduce the chance of the change actually becoming embedded into practice'.

My experience would be that directive change would be difficult in terms of introducing a sustainable approach to Intensive Interaction. The range of measures that would be necessary to train, educate and change the practices of staff would be extensive under a directive approach. However, management and strategic support is increasingly important if Intensive Interaction is going to be disseminated in a supported, systemic and sustainable way within any organisation.

Professional issues

So rich, varied and extensive are the activities and the outcomes of Intensive Interaction that different people could initially be attracted to the approach for differing reasons. In rather simplistic divisions, for example: parents and care workers for the relationship elements, speech and language therapists for the communication elements, education staff for the learning and cognitive elements, psychologists for the emotional and cognitive elements, and occupational therapists for the activity and sensory elements.

The variety of activities and outcomes in Intensive Interaction can result in people not really having a clear picture of who is responsible for the dissemination within an organisation. I have been involved in services where the lead agencies are psychology, or speech and language therapy, or occupational therapy or teaching staff.

The professionally qualified (such as speech and language therapists) are expected to pursue continuing professional development and so they are potentially better placed through training budgets, special interest groups and access to specialist journals to learn about and disseminate effective approaches. Moreover, these professionals often have clinical responsibility for a number of localities and services so they are, potentially, in a good position to effect change across organisations. However, it is possible that this may lead to misunderstandings about who is responsible for the approach within the work place. For example, if Intensive Interaction is introduced, as in my case, by a speech and language therapist, there is a danger that it is then seen as a speech and language therapist role and therefore an 'expert' therapy rather than as part of day-to-day life and the responsibility of everyone who spends time with people who would benefit from it (Irvine, 2001).

It would appear to make sense that the people who take ownership of Intensive Interaction within the work place are the very people who are in a position to use the approach regularly. One of the beautiful things about Intensive Interaction is that as an approach it is so very easily accessible for most people and the most obvious way of working with people who were previously seen as unreachable: 'the greatest praise an innovation can receive is for people to say "This is obvious! Why didn't I think of it? It's so simple"' (Drucker, 1991: 17).

And yet, there is a strange paradox in the Intensive Interaction community of practice in that, according to the organiser's participation lists, over 75 per cent of people attending the annual Intensive Interaction conferences from 2006 to 2010 were people with professional qualifications, and I suspect this is reflected in the people who attend regional support groups and those who are successful in getting funding for accredited training. The fact that many of the professionals attending the support network events return to their work place and offer support to people using Intensive Interaction on a daily basis is reassuring, but still leaves Intensive Interaction in the 'ownership' of the professionally qualified.

Perhaps some of the methods of propagation in professional journals involving research and technical terminology, though necessary to validate the approach, have been written in a style that is inaccessible to many readers and potential practitioners.

People approach Intensive Interaction from different standpoints. Some people are keen to practice immediately, needing nothing more than a basic introduction and help with reflective practice. Other people enjoy intellectualising the approach in studying underlying theories, concepts and rationales. Support mechanisms need to be accessible for both types of people; indeed, Intensive Interaction works technically in both of these ways.

Whatever the preferred style of support, empowering practitioners to take responsibility for their own practice, reflection and evaluation will surely increase the likelihood of sustainable practice.

In my work with new practitioners I constantly have in mind Carl Rogers's (1969) ideas on successful adult learning. These fit ideally with the underlying theories and practices of Intensive Interaction and encourage people to undertake the deep learning required for taking responsibility for their own practice. I will summarise some of Rogers's theories which I find most pertinent to the dissemination and teaching of Intensive Interaction.

Rogers's theories include the thoughts that learning is easier if the learners:

1 are encouraged to take responsibility for their own learning

2   provide much of the input for the learning so that deeper under-
    standing occurs through their own reflections, insights and
    experiences

3   learn to appreciate that the most valuable evaluation is self-eval-
    uation

4   focus on factors that are relevant to the learner and contribute to
    solving problems and/or achieving results.

In terms of people learning about and using Intensive Interaction,
this thinking may include activities like choosing the person they
want to interact with while learning about the approach, reflecting
on video recordings of themselves interacting, encouraging discussion about issues with tutor and colleagues, and evaluating progress
in both themselves and their interactive partner.

Alongside how learning happens are thoughts about the style of educator. These include:

1   not being protective of their constructs and beliefs

2   more able to listen to learners, especially to their feelings

3   pay as much attention to their relationship with learners as to the
    content of the course

4   able to accept feedback, both positive and negative, and to use it
    as insight into themselves and their behaviour/style.

In terms of teaching Intensive Interaction this means trainers who
are able to build good rapport and relationships with the learners.
Good listening skills are essential, as is being open to and honest
about difficult questions and sharing personal experience of Intensive Interaction (including difficulties while initially learning about
the approach). Rather than imparting knowledge as an 'expert' a
trainer would be prepared to have knowledge that is mutually constructed by the participants in a course.

National strategic issues

People reading this book are likely to be those who are already
involved in the use of Intensive Interaction and may wonder why
national strategic issues are relevant to themselves as practitioners.
However, if Intensive Interaction dissemination means making the
approach sustainably available to all who would benefit there are
some issues that need to be addressed:

How do parents hear about Intensive Interaction? I have introduced the approach to a variety of parents and the overwhelming feedback I get along with the gratitude is anger that they had to wait so long for something so effective.

How does Intensive Interaction break into the world of autism? Every practitioner who has used the approach with someone on the autism spectrum knows how effective it is but Intensive Interaction is still largely unrecognised and not recommended by many specialist autism services in their apparent preference for more autism-specific, often directive and well-marketed approaches. It is usually these specialist autism services that parents turn to once their child has been diagnosed, so the Intensive Interaction community of practice (see Graham Firth's discussions elsewhere in this volume) has a responsibility to ensure that the approach is represented and available to parents.

How do schools, adult services and parents employing personal assistants know that the person they are interviewing really knows about and are confident and effective in their practice of Intensive Interaction? How do services wishing to provide a package of training in Intensive Interaction know that what they will pay for will be effective? How can practitioners be reassured that what they are doing is really Intensive Interaction and how can these, possibly isolated, practitioners be supported? How can Intensive Interaction be implemented in private services in a way that enhances individual's lives?

The inclusion of Intensive Interaction in *Valuing People Now* (DoH, 2009) was reassuring, but the approach remains a recommendation rather than a directive and organisations have no obligation to train and support staff in using the approach. Indeed, an edict to use the approach would be difficult since the Intensive Interaction community of practice has been a rather fluid entity and to whom could government advisers have turned to if seeking guidance for the wider implementation of Intensive Interaction?

☐ Summary

Briefly then, to summarise and conclude. It is questions such as those that prompted the inauguration of the Intensive Interaction Institute in 2006 and yet, here is another paradox in the world of Intensive Interaction and its sense of 'fit' within organisations: how does the institute tackle these issues without being as well-packaged and protective as some other approaches have had to be in order to ensure dissemination and support of the approach in its true form? Rigidity and protectiveness does not fit easily with Intensive Interaction as an approach that is free-flowing, natural and spontaneous.

The answer must, perhaps, stay with the diffusive and participative models of change which are, by nature, slow. Five years after the creation of the Intensive Interaction Institute there is now an annual conference, regional support groups, regular study weekends, accredited Intensive Interaction coordinators training, an Assessed Practitioner course, regular newsletters, a publishing house (Face to Face) and an official website. The wider community of practice is, and will continue to be, a driving force in the dissemination and support of Intensive Interaction within organisations, but these measures are intended to keep the process truly participative.

References

Barber, M. (2007) 'Imitation, interaction and dialogue using Intensive Interaction: tea party rules', *British Journal of Support for Learning*, 22(3): 124–30.

Barber, M. (2008) 'Using Intensive Interaction to add to the palette of interactive possibilities in teacher–pupil communication', *European Journal of Special Needs Education*, 23(4): 393–402.

Crabbe, M. (2007) 'The Intensive Interaction research project … and beyond', *Royal College of Speech and Language Therapy Bulletin*, August: 12–13.

Department of Health (DoH) (2009) *Valuing People Now: A New Three-Year Strategy for People with Learning Disabilities*: www.dh.gov.uk/en/Publicationsandstatistics/Publications/PublicationsPolicyandGuidance/DH_093375 (accessed January 2011).

Drucker, P.F. (1991) 'The discipline of innovation', in J. Henry and D. Walker (eds), *Managing Innovation*. London: Sage Publications.

Elgie, S. and Maguire, N. (2001) 'Intensive Interaction with a woman with multiple and profound disabilities: a case study', *Tizard Learning Disability Review*, 6(3): 18–24.

Ellis, M. and Astell, A. (2008) 'A new approach to communicating with people with advanced dementia: a case study of adaptive interaction', in M.S. Zeedyk (ed.), *Promoting Social Interaction for Individuals with Communicative Impairments: Making Contact*. London: Jessica Kingsley.

Firth, G. (2008) 'A dual aspect process model of Intensive Interaction', *British Journal of Learning Disabilities*, 37: 43–9.

Firth, G. and Barber, M. (2010) *How to Use 'Intensive Interaction' with a Person with a Social or Communicative Impairment*. London: Jessica Kingsley.

Greenhalgh, T., Robert, G., MacFarlane, F., Bate, P. and Kyriakidou, O. (2004) 'Diffusion of innovations in service organisations: systematic review and recommendations', *The Milbank Quarterly*, 82(4): 581–629.

Hersey, P. and Blanchard, K. (1972) 'Change and the use of power: the management of change, part I', *Training and Development Journal*, 26(1): 6–10.

Hewett, D. and Nind, M. (1988) 'Developing an interactive curriculum for pupils with severe and complex learning difficulties', in B. Smith (ed.), *Interactive Approaches to the Education of Children with Severe Learning Difficulties*. Birmingham: Westhill College.

Irvine, C. (1998) 'Addressing the needs of adults with profound and multiple learning disabilities in social services provision', in D. Hewett and M. Nind (eds), *Interaction in Action*. London: David Fulton.

Irvine, C. (2001) 'On the floor and playing …', *Royal College of Speech and Language Therapy Bulletin*, November: 9–11.

Kellett, M. (2004) 'Intensive Interaction in the inclusive classroom: using interactive pedagogy to connect with students who are hardest to reach', *Westminster Studies in Education*, 27(2): 175–88.

Knight, C. and Watson, J. (1990) *Intensive Interaction Teaching at Gogarburn School*. Edinburgh: Moray House College.

Kotter, J. and Hesketh, J.L. (2008) *Corporate Culture and Performance*. New York: Free Press.

Nind, M. (2006) 'Beyond access to communication', keynote speech, Intensive Interaction Conference, 13 June, Leeds.

Nind, M. and Hewett, D. (1988) 'Interaction as curriculum', *British Journal of Special Education*, 15(2): 55–7.

Nind, M. and Hewett, D. (1994) *Access to Communication. Developing the Basics of Communication with People with Severe Learning Difficulties through Intensive Interaction*. London: David Fulton.

Nind, M. and Hewett, D. (2005) *Access to Communication. Developing the Basics of Communication with People with Severe Learning Difficulties through Intensive Interaction*, 2nd edn. London: David Fulton.

Rogers, C.R. (1969) *Freedom to Learn*. Columbus, OH: Merrill.

Rosenfeld, R. and Servo, J.C. (1990) 'Facilitating innovation in large organizations', in M.A. West and J. Farr (eds), *Innovation and Creativity at Work: Psychological and Organizational Strategies*. Chichester: Wiley.

Samuel, J. (2001) 'Intensive Interaction', *Clinical Psychology Forum*, 148: 22–5.

Somekh, B., Norman, A., Shannon, B. and Abbot, G. (1987) 'Action research in development', *Classroom Action Research Network*, Bulletin 8, Cambridge Institute of Education.

Zeedyk, M.S., Davies, C.E., Parry, S. and Caldwell, P. (2009) 'Fostering social engagement in Romanian children with communicative impairments: the experiences of newly trained practitioners of Intensive Interaction', *British Journal of Learning Disabilities*, 37(3): 186–96.

9

What is Intensive Interaction? Curriculum, process and approach

Dave Hewett

Chapter overview

More than 20 years ago, but about five years after the beginning of our work on the development of Intensive Interaction, I was verbally scolded by a university tutor, a then eminent educationist. He was considering one of our research proposals. He upbraided me at some length and with more irritation than I felt was justified or polite, because I had pronounced that Intensive Interaction was a good example of a 'process curriculum'. I cannot remember the detail of his argument, but it boiled down to 'no it is not'. In this chapter I continue that discussion, and once again make some (hopefully more learned) pronouncements about what Intensive Interaction is.

Intensive Interaction and process curricula

I now agree with that eminent educationist that Intensive Interaction is not a good example of a 'process curriculum'. It is not one first because it does not fully subscribe to the descriptions of a 'process curriculum' that were available in 1987. There was the rationale available from Bruner (1960) which, while eloquent and influential, remains brief and general. Bruner's formulation referred interestingly also to the concept of a 'spiral curriculum', which, along with Stern et al. (1977) has had some direct influence on the thinking set out here. There was also a brief reference to a process curriculum in Eisner (1985), one to which Intensive Interaction could only vaguely conform. Mainly however, there was the wide-ranging and still often referenced proposal of a 'process model of curriculum' from Stenhouse (1975). I feel that the development of Intensive Interaction has some sort of relationship with Stenhouse's rationale. This is the case both in theory and in the reality of the unfolding thinking of we practitioners brought up in the age of Stenhouse and his work near to us in and around East Anglia and Cambridge.

Secondly, it is not one because as a curriculum, Intensive Interaction just does not seem grand enough. The aspirations and intentions of Intensive Interaction are particular and not too general. The learning that is brought about is the most crucial learning for all people, but it is, in the first place at least, not too general, indeed rather focused in its scope. Intensive Interaction does not seem to conform to my favourite definition: 'A school's curriculum consists of all those activities designed or encouraged within its organisational framework to promote the intellectual, personal, social and physical development of its pupils' (DES, 1985: para. 11).

Reading about curriculum is an enjoyable minefield and I even surprise myself by finding the Department of Education and Science (DES) definition to be the one which I find most assimilable and usable. Just as an aside, I find myself frequently making the following statement. The learners for whom Intensive Interaction is crucial, far from needing a broad and balanced curriculum, instead need one that is rather particular and focused. The *National Curriculum General Guidelines for Learning Difficulties* (QCDA, 2008a) make this point rather clearly, but it seems to be lost or ignored in many of the special schools I visit.

I have increasingly not been using the word 'curriculum' alongside 'Intensive Interaction' despite citing the whole phrase in previous writings (for example, Nind and Hewett, 1988). That first journal article on Intensive Interaction was, perhaps somewhat ambitiously, entitled 'Interaction as curriculum'. However, as I remember it, the intention of the title was as much to refer to the exciting prospect of interactive process teaching and learning within the curriculum, as to giving any form of official title to the curriculum. The term 'process curriculum' was offered within the text though. Intensive Interaction is, I contend however, a good example of a process 'something'.

So what is it then? Defining Intensive Interaction as a teaching/learning approach

Much of what will be outlined in this section has been set out elsewhere – I must especially mention and recommend the milestone work by Collis and Lacey (1996) on interactive/process approaches. However, one of the pleasing aspects of the planning for this chapter was that I would try to bring various strands together into one narrative. I hope also to have ventured further.

Process-central approaches and emergence

There is a good question often asked by those practitioners who have a more technical orientation: 'Okay, Intensive Interaction is not an objectives-based approach to teaching. How does it work then?' It is tempting to answer something along the lines of 'well, it doesn't matter, Intensive Interaction is beautifully simple, just do it'. However, these things do matter, and I am always conscious of the need to reassure those who find it a daunting prospect to work with a, for them, new and apparently radical teaching approach, that the technicality of its workings is understood. The brief answer is that Intensive Interaction is what I think we can now call a 'process-central' approach. In this model, the learning outcomes gradually emerge over time, as a result of the rolling, cumulative, generative process of frequent, regular, repetitive activities of Intensive Interaction. The process is active when the two participants are engaged with each other and sharing a flow of enjoyable and interesting behaviour. The activities are live, active, meaningful rehearsals of the arts, skills, techniques, expertise, concepts, and so on, of being a communicator, carried out by the learner in partnership with someone who is already expert.

It may not be possible to be precise about when all the learning outcomes emerge. There is a sense of them gradually becoming visible in the communication performance of the learner within, or as a result of, the process.

The teaching, moment by moment, is more by a sense of artistry than by prescription, though the teaching operates within a framework or structure that is shared by teacher and learner. The teacher's moment-by-moment tactical decisions are informed by tuning-in minutely to the feedback signals of the learner and taking the processes of the learner fully into account. The teacher thus constructs the content and the flow of the activity mainly by responding to the behaviour of the learner. The most frequently seen response is imitation/joining-in/copying.

It seems to me that there is nothing particularly radical about the proposition of emergent outcomes outlined above. The approach to learning described within the Early Years Foundation Stage (EYFS) (QCDA, 2008b) surely advocates working in just this way – with emergent learning outcomes. The emphasis of the EYFS is on the daily provision of a congregation of beneficial developmental experiences where play 'underpins the delivery of all the EYFS' (QCDA, 2008b: 7). There is little emphasis on prescriptive or objectives-dominated activities; rather emphasis is on the processes of learning the children will undergo during their daily experience of the congregation of beneficial activities. The EYFS does outline full descriptions of the intended learning outcomes or 'Early Learning Goals', but looks to these outcomes to arise and emerge from the activities, rather than the activities to drive towards them. There is thus great stress within the EYFS on the technical proficiency of members of staff – planning, being play partners, responding to individual needs, being observant, evaluating, assessing and recording.

The point here is that with this vision of emergent outcomes, one is not taken by surprise. These are not unplanned or random outcomes; these are the intended outcomes of the provision of activities, described in advance of the provision of the activities. It is simply that the learning outcomes are not the driving force of every activity as in a linear, objective-orientated model. The more recent EYFS document (QCDA, 2009) is even more explicit in describing the central-process nature of play within the approaches to teaching and learning.

There is a noble history of previous attempts to describe the pertinent teaching. The apparently creative, spontaneous, but informed teaching techniques have been given luminous phrases such as: 'flexible purposing' (Dewey, 1910), 'teachable moments' (attributed to Havighurst, 1952, but may go as far back as Pestalozzi in 1898), then 'teaching by artistry' and, yes, 'emergent ends' (Eisner, 1985). There is also Vygotsky and the zone of proximal development (ZPD).

Vygotsky and the ZPD

Here, I must acknowledge Verenikina (2003) for her review of the interpretations of Vygotsky's formulations. Later, I shall refer briefly to dynamic systems perspective and its potential relationship to Intensive Interaction. Such theories I offer, give us a structure for being comfortable with the reality that we cannot possibly con-sciously comprehend all of the workings of the teaching and learning within Intensive Interaction. Similarly, the zone of proximal development and the scaffolding metaphor have always seemed to be useful thinking tools for allowing for the complexity of the teach-ing operation within parent–infant interaction and Intensive Interaction. Scaffolding and the ZPD are thus envisaged here as something rather more extensive than the often rather mechanistic interpretations available in texts linking Vygotsky to classroom prac-tice. Stone (1998: 360) warns of these potential 'limitations of the scaffolding metaphor' and Verenikina elaborates the theme:

> Thus, to understand the complexity of ZPD, it is necessary to take into account such concepts as tool mediation, social mediation of learning, internalisation, intersubjectivity and the active position of the child in learning. When we talk about working in the zone of proximal development, we look at the way that a child's performance is mediated socially, that is, how shared understanding or intersubjectivity has been achieved. (2003: 5)

Some writers on Intensive Interaction, for example Firth (2010), have visualised the ZPD operating within the approach. Let us go further. In Intensive Interaction, the ZPD surely presents itself in Verenikina's purest sense in order fully to account for the sense of teacher 'artistry' already mentioned. It is a social instrument. It is a mal-leable, flexible, questing entity, constantly reforming itself around or ahead of the sensibilities and gathering powers of the learner. The scaffolding of the teacher is similarly fluid, never static, energised to all the contingencies of the learning situation. In Intensive Interac-tion, this is rarely a planned operation; the scaffolding performance is largely extemporised, a great part of the teacher's actions being intuitive and tacit, not necessarily conscious, but also judiciously blended with the conscious, tactical decisions. This is a much more organic, more gestalt vision of scaffolding than say, itemising a list of useful ways to carry out scaffolding, as in McDevitt and Ormrod (2002, cited in Verenikina, 2003). 'Scaffolding' is thus for me a vivid, workable description of part of the pedagogy of this process-central approach and central to its operation.

Outcomes, complexity and dynamic systems

In parent–infant interaction and Intensive Interaction, the learning is so vast and complex, the expert cannot break it down into sequen-tial steps, cannot even consciously comprehend everything she or he knows. Rather, the complex learning situation gradually makes avail-able the transfer of everything the expert does know, and also provides the dynamic social ecology necessary for the development of the cognitive substructures for the learner. So, what do I mean by cognitive substructures?

When discussing Intensive Interaction, it is important never to stray too far from reference to the teaching intentions and outcomes. Any rationale of Intensive Interaction must include an unremitting focus on the learning outcomes, usually expressed as the fundamentals of communication (FOCs) (Nind and Hewett, 1994) as seen in Figure 9.1. In initial training sessions, I have gradually increased time spent discussing the FOCs in order to place more and more emphasis on the 'why'. I suggest that accepting the critical importance of the learning intentions is especially necessary for this approach. This awareness assists practitioners with the acceptance of the repetitive aspects of the process of teaching and learning which will be discussed later.

- **Enjoying being with another person**

- **Developing the ability to attend to that person**

- **Concentration and attention span**

- **Learning to do sequences of activity with another person**

- **Taking turns in exchanges of behaviour**

- **Sharing personal space**

- **Using and understanding eye contacts**

- **Using and understanding facial expressions**

- **Using and understanding physical contacts**

- **Using and understanding other non-verbal communications**

- **Vocalising and using vocalisations meaningfully (including speech)**

- **Learning to regulate and control arousal levels**

- **Fundamental emotional learning**

- **(Probably) the development of neural links**

Figure 9.1 The fundamentals of communication

The list in Figure 9.1 has its origin in the same place as Intensive Interaction, drawing on the vast literature and research on parent–infant interaction and borrowing some of its terminology. This has been the standard rationale for the learning outcomes for some time, though I have recently added to it, or rather the work of Intensive Interaction practitioners and writers has caused me to amend it. There are some observations about this list that are important and which contribute to the nature of our understanding of Intensive Interaction as a teaching approach.

First, this list is a compromise, a sketch of the outcomes. It is a bit, well, sketchy. By that I mean that it is not a full description of the learning outcomes. This list merely describes some of the visible behaviours that are the performances of a communicator. It is therefore a 'tip of the iceberg' observation. Surely, we can all visualise that this is a tiny proportion of the learning that has taken place. The vast mass, the bulk of the learning takes place in, resides within, the learner's brain. These visible performances arise because that learning has taken place. Figure 9.2 attempts to provide a simple visualisation of this state of affairs.

This aspect of theorising is admittedly a little theoretical. It is difficult to demonstrate the existence of the cognitive substructures, though cognitive psychology mostly takes it as a given that learning results in and is supported by cognitive schemata or other similar units of 'organized knowledge about events, situations or objects' (Elliot et al., 1996: 243). However, I find that nearly everyone who studies the diagram seems successfully to relate to it from their own experience of their own brains. I must also cite the conceptual influence of an 'interactive developmental paradigm' (Levine et al., 1993) and their vision of the arrays of 'elemental functions' that underpin learning and performance.

As can be seen, the substructures may literally include neural hardware. Elsewhere in this volume (Chapter 4), M. Suzanne Zeedyk has reviewed the evidence on the link between the dynamic interpersonal nature of parent–infant interactions and the growth of neural links in the infant brain. At present, it is something of a leap to state that the same happens for older learners. However, we already know that older learners nonetheless conduct much of this complex learning.

Thus, a central issue is that the nature of these learning outcomes fundamentally and inextricably relates to the teaching and learning processes that bring them about; the processes of taking part in the learning are also some of the learning outcomes. In natural development, the learning of the first two years or so, particularly the central themes of learning to relate, interact, communicate and then use language, this is probably the most complicated learning in life. Actually, it is complicated beyond the ability of any of us to comprehend its constituent parts. The substructure components cannot be seen, we cannot name them, we can only have this vague comprehension of their existence. Yet they are the major aspect of the learning.

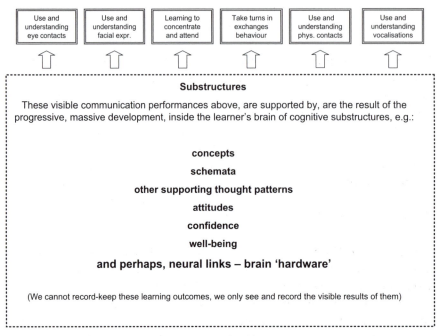

Figure 9.2 Visible learning outcomes and substructure outcomes

Thus Figure 9.2 attempts to encapsulate this or to promote a range of realisations in the mind of the reader. Please try to visualise attempting to teach the vastness of the cognitive substructures by using our more 'traditional' teaching approaches. Consider carrying out a task analysis on use and understanding of eye contacts, facial expressions and physical contacts. Yes, there may have been attempts to operantly train some of those performances, but these attempts are few and fell away amongst the general acceptance that behavioural methods are not adequate for teaching the labrynthine complexities of communication cognitions and performances, a point 'not even contested by most behaviourists' (Hewett and Nind, 1998). That is one reason why Intensive Interaction is not objectives-based learning, and why content analysis is not a major issue in the provision of learning through Intensive Interaction. There is an implicit acceptance that the content of the learning is complex beyond analysis.

Despite its admittedly rather primitive appearance, I think the diagram has helped me to think about and convey these understandings about teaching and learning. In my early years as a teacher, I was steeped in the use of behavioural approaches (see Hewett, 1989; Nind and Hewett, 1994). Taking part in the development work on Intensive Interaction was partly an expression of my dissatisfaction with their adequacy. I cannot claim at that time to have been a knowledgeable anti-behaviourist, simply dissatisfied.

I think I now understand that behavioural approaches we have traditionally used will perhaps attempt operantly to train a person to produce the visible behaviours in the boxes along the top. A behavioural approach is not likely to place the learner in rich, dynamic, complex learning situations where the cognitive substructures are gradually developed. This therefore, might also explain the well-documented problems of 'stick' and 'generalisation' with behavioural approaches.

Figure 9.3 attempts to represent the thoughts expressed in the previous four paragraphs. I started using this diagram several years ago as a hopefully amusing, wry observation and a stimulus to discussion with groups. I think the message of the diagram is clear, but two things need to be borne in mind. First, do not try to decipher the upper drawing too much, it is an entirely schematic representation of what my brain feels like when I am communicating. In fact, it is a simplification; I think my communicator's mind is much more elaborate and complex than that. Secondly, I hope most readers will relate to the very linear fashion of teaching suggested in the lower drawing (Figure 9.3b). Attempts at controlled, task analysis-type teaching always feel like that to me.

Surely, most of our education system tries to work in that way, and it certainly seems to be the most commonly seen type of approach in special education. This chapter takes its place in a long history of reservations querying the reliance on this model and its adequacy. Vrasidas's (2000) critique traces this general tradition to Tyler (1949) who he cites as being the father of the 'linear model of curriculum development' and instrumental in promulgating general behaviourist learning theories. There are less temperate observations. Recent notable authoritative observations are von Glaserfeld (1996) for the vehemence of the critique, and Bruner (2004) for the jocular dismissiveness toward behavioural approaches.

Nonetheless let us be clear, despite all previous comments, I am in no way dismissing the use of the linear, objectivist or behaviourist approach to teaching and learning. Proponents of 'interactive' approaches are often particular to make this point (for example, Berry, 2010; Collis and Lacey, 1996; Nind, 2000; Nind and Hewett, 1994). Certain things can be usefully taught by these methods. We do however, strongly advocate a properly technical appreciation of 'horses for courses' in teaching approaches. In that light, the main obvious suggestion of the diagram is that the teaching approach in Figure 9.3b will not do for the performances and learning in Figure 9.3a.

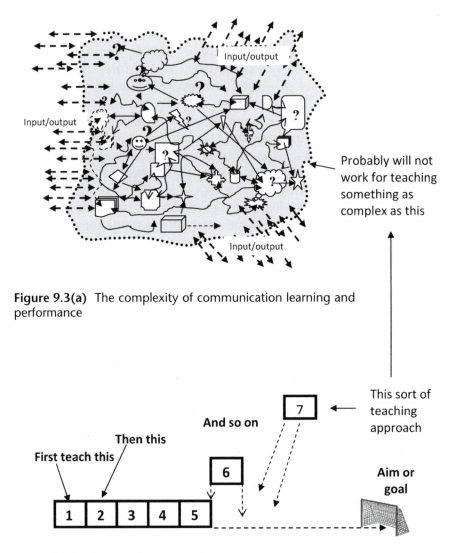

Figure 9.3(a) The complexity of communication learning and performance

Figure 9.3(b) How we like to teach

As I used it with groups, I gradually began to view the diagram more seriously and included it in an article on play (Hewett, 2006). It seems logical that Intensive Interaction may also be viewed as an example of play-based learning, in that the activities are largely, but not wholly, playful. I am therefore interested in play and play-based learning. I have always been impressed by the observation of Tharp and Gallimore (1988) that if you think about it, by the time that children go to school (usually around 6 years old in the USA), they have already learnt all of the most important and the most complicated things they will learn in their lives. These things are learnt due to what they term, 'natural teaching': 'In every culture, natural teaching transmits skills of immense variety and power – a "curriculum" of far greater complexity than anything attempted in schools' (Tharp and Gallimore, 1988: 20).

Tharp and Gallimore make two further points about the natural curriculum. First, it is remarkable how little of the practices of it influence schooling, instructional programmes and curriculum design, even though the teaching and learning within it of very important and complicated things is mostly successful for most people. Secondly, 'higher order cognitive and linguistic skills' are naturally learnt 'within the pleasures of the social interaction'. As I, among so many others (Hewett, 2006) including even the QCDA (2009), have pointed out, play is an intrinsic aspect of early learning, of the natural curriculum, and 'Play is actually a complex, multi-layered, multi-faceted situation that is just right for learning things that are like that' (Hewett, 2006: 8). Play can, of course, be used as a teaching and learning technique within task-orientated activities but, surely, classically, learning through play is process-central learning.

So, my central points here are: communication learning is the most significant aspect of the 'natural' curriculum. The learning of human communication is complex and multifaceted beyond our ability to consciously comprehend all its intricacies and constituent parts. Intensive Interaction sessions at their best feel simple and beautiful to the participants, but they are actually complex and multifaceted as in Figure 9.3a. The teaching of communication through Intensive Interaction therefore embodies the acceptance that the activities cause learning outcomes that we cannot see nor name, nor even properly conceptualise. This is not a problem; it seems likely that we should never be able to deconstruct these complexities into constituent parts. Nor should we. This seems to be precisely what takes place in the natural model of parent–infant interaction.

The fields of developmental psychology, learning theory, curriculum and pedagogy are still at the early stages of embracing this dynamic blend of cognitivist and social constructivist conceptualisation of early learning and development. Twelve years ago (Hewett and Nind, 1998) I chronicled the promise held out by the work of researchers in the USA who were looking at human development through the focus of dynamic systems perspective or 'chaos theory' (Fogel and Thelen, 1987). Progress has been somewhat hesitant, though still promising. Smith and Thelen comment on the relatively slow forward movement of their own work, and that of others:

> But only in the past decade or so have the concepts and models of non-linear dynamic systems made in-roads into traditional developmental psychology, becoming a contender for a new developmental theory and fundamentally changing the way development is studied. Developmental psychologists have used dynamic systems ideas both as a conceptual theory and in various formal mathematical treatments of developmental change. (2003: 343)

Dynamic systems perspective seems to offer the prospect of a general theory which can ultimately embrace the issues arising in Figure 9.3. Dynamic systems or chaos theorists are comfortable with not being able to describe and identify all active parts of dynamic systems (Fogel et al., 2008). They hold non-linearity in development as a given (Thelen, 2005) and outcomes emergence as obvious in dynamic systems (Fogel, 2006; Smith and Thelen, 2003). Of the major proponents, Thelen (2005) has been more interested in general development than the particularities of communication learning, though Fogel (2006), while recently focusing on 'social communication' and the development of self and emotion, has consistently applied his work to the study of parent–infant interaction.

However, I am not necessarily proposing that Intensive Interaction becomes defined for instance as a 'dynamic systems perspective model of teaching and learning'. More that these theories hold out the prospect of a general rationale for Intensive Interaction as a complex model where not all aspects of its enactment are precisely understood. What is understood is the array of actions available to the teacher as facilitator for instigating the workings of the system with the learner.

The three 'R's and 'spiralling'

I offer one last piece of theory in support of downright practicalities. It is a handy, maybe somewhat gimmicky phrase when introducing Intensive Interaction to practitioners, to emphasise that it has three 'R's. These are simply, 'Responsiveness', 'Repetition' and 'Repertoire'. Again, these words or terms are borrowed from the parent–infant interaction literature, particularly, with some license, from Tiffany Field's (1978) poetically entitled, 'The three Rs of infant–adult interactions: rhythms, repertoires, and responsivity'. This little gimmick is, I think, a friendly way of giving great emphasis to the necessity for repetition. Teachers in schools especially, need fully to grasp that if the totality of the progress that any individual can make is to be anywhere near attained, the activities need to be repeated literally many, many times, day by day. This orientation to Intensive Interaction as a means to long-term development for the individual places such an outlook firmly within what Graham Firth nominates as a 'developmental process model' (Firth, Chapter 7, this volume).

During training workshops, I find it useful to make the allusion to the natural model on this issue, to show a mother and a baby of three months in interaction and ask the audience to consider, in anything like optimum circumstances, how many thousands of repetitions of these types of activity, this baby will have on a daily, weekly basis throughout the first two years. This point was richly emphasised at the earliest stages of parent–infant interaction research (see Schaffer, 1977, and other contributors in that volume). And, on a day-by-day basis, as a result of the repetition of the activities, to consider how the activities gradually expand. They gradually expand in duration, they gradually expand in content and they gradually expand in sophistication and complexity – simply through the main engine-room of that repetition. That is how it works with babies. We dress it up with scientific theorising of course, but when it is going well for the participants, it just happens and it feels as simple as that.

This aspect of the approach can seem a problematic prospect to practitioners. Teachers in their, for instance, highly organised special school classrooms, can struggle to visualise how the classroom will reorganise so that some of the learners can have frequent, regular Intensive Interaction activities. Accordingly, I suspect that it can be rare for a child to receive the intensity of input that she or he might actually be able to accommodate.

Additionally, practitioners are often not psychologically adjusted to this degree of repetition of activities. Rather, they are often experiencing external pressures constantly to move on, to get the learner urgently to the next stage. Most teachers I work with seem to agree with the observation that we do not do enough repetition of activities, enough consolidation of where the learner is 'at', as an integral part of the process of moving them on.

I think there is also the understandable desire among often the more knowledgeable practitioners to be eclectic in their practices, taking some of the best aspects of this approach, some of that and so on. This is an apparently shrewd observation I hear frequently from classroom teachers. It can then feel to them to be less than eclectic to 'clear the decks' somewhat and have a commitment to these communication activities above all else, for the learners who need them. It can smack of an ideological commitment they had hitherto been avoiding. Worse, that commitment brings with it the obvious prospect of that wholesale reorganisation of the classroom and the timetable.

Once again, reference to the parent–infant interaction research has provided inspiration for a model to assist. The use of the term 'spiral' or 'spiralling' is frequently used in various fields of human endeavour to imply a pattern of progress or moving forward positively. It occurs in the parent–infant research literature also. For many years our work on Intensive Interaction has borrowed and developed the image, inviting practitioners to visualise that the activities gradually 'lift off' and 'spiral upwards' with a sense of the success in the activities breeding further success and so on.

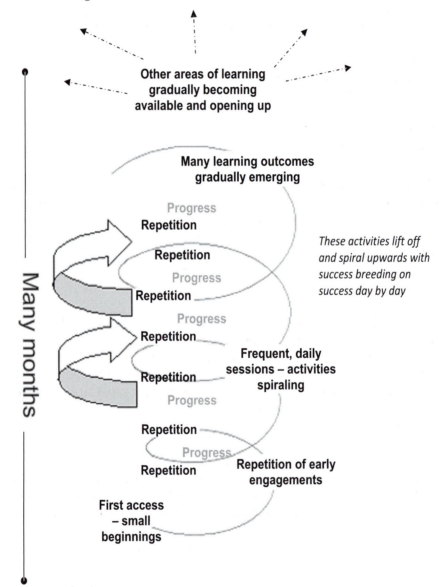

Figure 9.4 Parent–infant interaction and Intensive Interaction work like this – 'spiralling'

Figure 9.4 employs the concept of the spiral to illustrate the extreme non-linear nature of the development of Intensive Interaction activities and the outcomes. It also offers a shape that can embody repetition of activities and consolidation of that which is learnt. In fact, Figure 9.4 is not quite right for me. I would visualise the loops of the spiral being flatter, more densely packed, more gradually ascending with plenty of looping around the same spot; I have drawn this by hand, but something like the spiral in Figure 9.5. This diagram shows the repetitions growing from small beginnings, the loops of the repetitions travelling wider as the repertoire expands, the overall dedication to continued repetition throughout the process. It also displays that the process is onwards and upwards. However, within my crude diagram, perhaps there is tolerance also for the prospect of staying in one place, on one loop of the spiral for a while. Even, perhaps, spiralling down a few loops to an already safely established place during times of stress or adverse circumstances for the person.

Figure 9.5 Flatter spiral

So, I hope I have displayed elegant style in drawing to a close by returning to a concept mentioned at the beginning – Bruner and the spiral curriculum. Intensive Interaction is still not a spiral curriculum, but the spiral shape feels a totally more apt description of the process of long-term development than anything linear. I like this shape. I hope this conceptualisation will serve to assist practitioners everywhere to become comfortable and indeed determined to give the whole process of development through Intensive Interaction the repetitive energy that is necessary. It is certainly my intention that the spiral should remind all of us who write about, disseminate or manage practitioners carrying out the approach, that we must motivate and reassure front-line staff accordingly.

☐ Summary

I have set out to place Intensive Interaction within theories about what we do in our field and describe a usable technical rationale for the intricacies of the teaching and learning. I suggest that in order to do this it is necessary to extend present theorising somewhat to the proposition of a 'process-central' approach. The nature of 'emergent outcomes' is a previously established concept, but one which is in my view insufficiently propounded even where it is richly recommended, such as in the EYFS. Similarly, the essence of a 'spiralling' model of outcomes and development was previously theoretically projected, and now provides a conceptual structure for the repetition of activities within such a process-central approach. Visualising Intensive Interaction as a true example of a 'dynamic system' in action can help practitioners to feel comfortable with the less tangible aspects of the teaching and learning and the fundamental nature of the divergence from linear/objectives models. The relationship between the thinking of Vygotsky and Intensive Interaction has been extended to the visualisation of the ZPD and scaffolding as intricate, dynamic social instruments critical to the operation of the process (or system) and the moment-by-moment extemporisation by the teacher at the centre of the process or system.

References

Berry, R. (2010) 'Some psychological theories of human behaviour', in R. Firth, R. Berry and C. Irving (eds), *Understanding Intensive Interaction*. London: Jessica Kingsley.

Bruner, J. (1960) *The Process of Education*. Cambridge, MA: Harvard University Press.

Bruner, J. (2004) 'A short history of psychological theories of learning', *Daedalus*, 133: 21–8.

Collis, M. and Lacey, P. (1996) *Interactive Approaches to Teaching: A Framework for INSET*. London: David Fulton.

Department of Education and Science (DES) (1985) *The Curriculum from 5 to 16: Curriculum Matters 2*. London: Her Majesty's Stationery Office.

Dewey, J. (1910) *How We Think*. Lexington, MA: D.C. Heath.

Eisner, E.W. (1985) *The Educational Imagination: On the Design and Development of School Programs*. New York: Macmillan.

Elliot, S.N., Kratochwill, J. and Travers, J.F. (1996) *Educational Psychology: Effective Teaching, Effective Learning*. Dubuque, IA: Brown and Benchmark Publishers.

Field, T. (1978) 'The three Rs of infant–adult interactions: rhythms, repertoires, and responsivity', *Journal of Pediatric Psychology*, 3(3): 131–6.

Firth, G. (2010) 'Issues associated with human learning (developmental issues)', in G. Firth, R. Berry and C. Irvine (eds), *Understanding Intensive Interaction: Context and Concepts for Professionals and Families*. London: Jessica Kingsley.

Fogel, A. (2006) 'Dynamic systems research on interindividual communication: the transformation of meaning-making', *The Journal of Developmental Processes*, 1: 7–30.

Fogel, A. and Thelen, E. (1987) 'Development of early expressive and communicative action: re-interpreting the evidence from a dynamic systems perspective', *Developmental Psychology*, 23(6): 747–61.

Fogel, A., Greenspan, S., King, B.J., Lickliter, R., Reygadas, P., Shanker, S. and Toren, C. (2008) 'Dynamic systems methods for the life sciences', in A. Fogel, B.J. King and S. Shanker (eds), *Human Development in the Twenty-First Century: Visionary Ideas from Systems Scientists*. Cambridge: Cambridge University Press.

Glasersfeld, E. von (1995) 'A constructivist approach to teaching', in L.P. Steffe and J. Gale (eds), *Constructivism in Education*. Hillsdale, NJ: Lawrence Erlbaum.

Havighurst, R.J. (1952) *Human Development and Education*. New York: Longman.

Hewett, D. (1989) 'The most severe learning difficulties: does your curriculum go back far enough?', in M. Ainscow (ed.), *Special Education in Change*. London: David Fulton.

Hewett, D. (2006) 'The most important and complicated learning: that's what play is for!', *ICAN Talking Point*, March, www.talkingpoint.org.uk, viewed October 2007, PDF available from daveinteract@hotmail.com

Hewett, D. and Nind, M. (1998) 'Future developments', in D. Hewett and M. Nind (eds), *Interaction in Action: Reflections on the Use of Intensive Interaction*. London: David Fulton.

Levine, M.D., Hooper, S., Montgomery, J., Reed, M., Sandler, A., Schwartz, C. and Watson, T. (1993) 'Learning disabilities: an interactive developmental paradigm', in G.R. Lyon (ed.), *Better Understanding Learning Disabilities: New Views from Research and Their Implications for Education and Public Policies*. Baltimore, MD: Paul H. Brookes.

McDevitt, T.M. and Ormrod, J.E. (2002) *Child Development and Education*. Upper Saddle River, NJ: Merrill Prentice Hall.

Nind, M. (2000) 'Teachers' understanding of interactive approaches in special education', *International Journal of Disability, Development and Education*, 47(2): 184–99.

Nind, M. and Hewett, D. (1988) 'Interaction as curriculum', *British Journal of Special Education*, 15(2): 55–7.

Nind, M. and Hewett, D. (1994) *Access to Communication*. London: David Fulton.

Pestalozzi, J.H. (1898) *Comment Gertrude Instruit Ses Enfants*. Paris: Lib C. Delagrave.

Qualifications and Curriculum Development Agency (QCDA) (2008a) *National Curriculum General Guidelines for Learning Difficulties*. London: Department for Children, Schools and Families.

Qualifications and Curriculum Development Agency (QCDA) (2008b) *Practice Guidance for the Early Years Foundation Stage.* London: Department for Children, Schools and Families.

Qualifications and Curriculum Development Agency (QCDA) (2009) *Learning, Playing and Interacting: Good Practice in the Early Years Foundation Stage.* London: Department for Children, Schools and Families.

Schaffer, H.R. (1977) 'Early interactive development', in H.R. Schaffer (ed.), *Studies in Mother–Infant Interaction.* London: Academic Press.

Smith, L.B. and Thelen, E. (2003) 'Development as a dynamic system', *TRENDS in Cognitive Sciences,* 7(8): 343–8.

Stenhouse, L. (1975) *An Introduction to Curriculum Research and Development.* London: Heinemann.

Stern, D.N., Beebe, B., Jaffe, J. and Bennet, S.L. (1977) 'The infant's stimulus world during social interaction: a study of caregiver behaviours with particular reference to repetition and timing', in H.R. Schaffer (ed.), *Studies in Mother–Infant Interaction.* New York: Academic Press.

Stone, C.A. (1998) 'The metaphor of scaffolding: its utility for the field of learning disabilities', *Journal of Learning Disabilities,* 3(4): 344–64.

Tharp, R. and Gallimore, R. (1988) *Rousing Minds to Life: Teaching, Learning, and Schooling in Social Context.* New York: Cambridge University Press.

Thelen, E. (2005) 'Motor development as foundation and future of developmental psychology', *International Journal of Behavioral Development,* 24(4): 385–97.

Tyler, R.W. (1949) *Basic Principles of Curriculum and Instruction.* Chicago, IL: University of Chicago Press.

Verenikina, I. (2003) 'Understanding scaffolding and the ZPD in educational research', *Conference Papers of AARE/NZARE,* Auckland.

Vrasidas, C. (2000) 'Constructivism versus objectivism: implications for interaction, course design, and evaluation in distance education', *International Journal of Educational Telecommunications,* 6(4): 339–62.

Author index

Subject index

Added to a page number 'f' denotes a figure.